BATTLE OF FALLING WATERS 1863

Custer, Pettigrew and the End of the Gettysburg Campaign

by

GEORGE F. FRANKS, III

Published by George F. Franks, III

For more information please contact us via email at:
fallingwatersmd1863@gmail.com

First Edition

ISBN: 1484138376
ISBN 13: 9781484138373

Library of Congress Control Number: 2013907803
CreateSpace Independent Publishing Platform, North Charleston,
South Carolina

PRINTED AND BOUND IN THE UNITED STATES OF AMERICA

To Melissa

For your vision, support, patience, encouragement and love.

Acknowledgements

While many people have encouraged my study of history and in particular, my passion for the American conflict of 1861 – 1865, often referred to as our Civil War, several people have played an important role during the ten years of research, writing, and editing of this book on the final battle of the Gettysburg Campaign.

First, to my editor and friend, Timothy Terrell, for his patience, professionalism and doggedness, as my editor and publishing adviser.

To Washington County Free Library's legendary John Frye of the Western Maryland Room for his guidance and support at the inception of this project.

To Scott Bragunier of the Williamsport, Maryland, Town Council for his leadership in establishing and managing the annual "Retreat Through Williamsport" commemoration including tours and talks related to the Battle of Falling Waters, Maryland.

To Jeffrey Brown for sharing his research on the Battle of Falling Waters, including the wonderful newspaper article about the return of the Confederate battle flag.

To my friends and fellow members of the Capitol Hill Civil War Round Table and the Hagerstown Civil War Round Table for their interest and encouragement.

To Mariel Yohe, for her timely technical support and editorial assistance.

To my parents, the late George F. Franks, Jr., and Mrs. Elizabeth L'Hote Franks Robin for encouraging my interest in history and the Civil War in particular through many summer vacations devoted to visiting battlefields, and museums, plus weekend trips to participate (as a young drummer boy) in North-South Skirmish Association events.

To my daughters, Abby Franks Melvin and Melissa Franks, for their love and support through the duration of this research and writing project which spanned their high school, college, and early professional years.

Finally, to my partner and the love of my life, Melissa Cooperson, without whom, literally, this project would never have started much less reached publication.

George F. Franks, III
Daniel Donnelly House (1830)
Williamsport, Maryland
April 2013

Table of Contents

List of Maps and Illustrations

Maps

Map 1. "Chasing Lee to the Potomac" (John Heiser, *Gettysburg Magazine*, Issue Number Eleven, p. 47).

Map 2. "Position of the Armies below Hagerstown, July 13, 1863" (John Heiser, *Gettysburg Magazine*, Issue Number Twenty-Two, p. 127).

Map 3. "Williamsport and Vicinity, July 1863" (John Heiser, *Gettysburg Magazine*, Issue Number Twenty-Seven, p. 87).

Map 4. Detail of the Falling Waters battlefield from "Map of the Vicinity of Hagerstown, Funkstown, Williamsport and Falling Waters, Md. Accompanying the Report of Major General G. G. Meade on the Battle of Gettysburg dated October 1st 1863" (Author's Collection).

Illustrations

Illustration 1. "Charge of the 6th Michigan cavalry over the rebel earthworks nr. Falling Waters," Alfred Waud, 1863 (Library of Congress).

Illustration 2. "Gallant charge by two companies of the 6th Michigan on Tuesday morning on the rebel rearguard, near Falling Waters ...," Edwin Forbes, 1863 (Library of Congress).

Illustration 3. Brig. Gen. J. Johnston Pettigrew (*Confederate Military History*, 1899).

Illustration 4. Brig. Gen. George A. Custer, 1863 (Library of Congress).

Introduction

The story of the Gettysburg Campaign, both before and after the July 1–3, 1863, battle, has recently received increased attention from historians. The movement of the Army of Northern Virginia from Gettysburg and its pursuit by the Army of the Potomac are every bit as important to the study of the American Civil War as the events in and around the small crossroads town in Pennsylvania. Many historians agree the Gettysburg Campaign concluded with the Battle of Falling Waters, Maryland, on July 14, 1863. Although not the climactic battle of the war desired by President Abraham Lincoln, it remains a story of miscalculation, bravery, and tragedy. This is the story of that final battle.

Chapter 1

July 4–12

Lee's Withdrawal to Williamsport, Maryland, and Meade's Pursuit

Following Army of Northern Virginia commander Gen. Robert E. Lee's grand assault in Gettysburg, Pennsylvania, on the afternoon of July 3, 1863, both armies withdrew behind their modest field fortifications and waited for the other to attack. The dead and the dying lay strewn across every field, hill, and gully. Homes, barns, churches, and schools in and around Gettysburg overflowed with wounded soldiers from both armies. The stench of dead men and horses filled the hot summer air and flies were thick and everywhere. Far from the relative safety of his base of supply and operations in Virginia, Lee was baffled that his current adversary, the Army of the Potomac's new commander, Maj. Gen. George G. Meade, did not follow up on his July 3 success with a counter attack on July 4.

Lee ordered Brig. Gen. John D. Imboden, a cavalry brigade commander, to escort a wagon train of wounded, prisoners, and captured supplies back to Virginia by way of the Falling Waters crossing south of Williamsport, Maryland. Word had not reached Lee his pontoon crossing over the Potomac River had been destroyed by a Union cavalry patrol. The Confederate wounded who could be moved in wagons, ambulances, and even on foot, would travel southward in advance of and on a different route than the main body of the Army of Northern

Virginia. Lee determined it was time to return to Virginia. His army had drawn the enemy out of Virginia and they had been able to live off the abundant resources of Maryland and Pennsylvania. They had captured or otherwise procured supplies and struck a blow to the enemy farther north than the previous September when they clashed with the Federals then under the command of Maj. Gen. George McClellan at Sharpsburg, Maryland.

As a portion of Lee's cavalry escorted the wounded on their trek back to Virginia the night of July 4, Meade evaluated his options. The Army of the Potomac had been badly mauled during the three days of brutal combat which had followed a campaign of pursuit beginning in Virginia the previous month. Meade's men and supplies were to a large degree spent. Tactically, his troops held the high ground around Gettysburg and he was pleased Lee had chosen not to follow up on his massive frontal assault of July 3. Meade received accolades via telegraph messages from the War Department in response to his initial reports about the battle. War-weary President Abraham Lincoln in Washington was buoyant. The victory at Gettysburg coincided with news of Maj. Gen. Ulysses S. Grant's capture of Vicksburg, Mississippi, on the western front of the war following a prolonged siege. For Lincoln and those who supported the Union cause, news of the two victories made July 4 an occasion for celebration beyond the usual festivities.

But Meade, a West Point graduate and military engineer just like his opponent Lee, was a very cautious man by nature unlike the bold and audacious Lee. He waited to see what Lee would do next. He had deferred to the guidance of his Council of War on the evening of July 2. He continued to listen to their opinions and recommendations as he pondered his next steps on July 4. The majority of Meade's subordinate field commanders made it clear their troops were in no condition to shift from a defensive fight to taking the offense against Lee's army, regardless of how badly it had been pummeled over the past days. So Meade waited and requested the War Department in Washington provide him with more men, more supplies, and more time. The Army of the Potomac's soldiers waited, as soldiers do the majority of their time, in and around Gettysburg. Heavy rain storms drenched the landscape, the unscathed, the wounded, and the cold, bloating bodies of dead men and horses.

In the heavy rain Imboden and his officers guided the seemingly endless wagon train of the wounded, prisoners, and spoils of war slowly toward the Potomac River crossing at Williamsport. Several elements of Imboden's withdrawal toward the Potomac are essential to the story of Falling Waters. First, rain and mud, in addition to treacherous mountain passes and roads, magnified the horror of the journey. Second, the citizens of central Pennsylvania and western Maryland were not, for the most part, favorable to the southerners or their cause. They saw Lee and his army as invaders and looters and the local farmers and other citizens responded accordingly. Supplies and forage were confiscated by the rebels both on their journey to and from Gettysburg and were paid for, in accordance with Lee's orders, but with their Confederate currency. Third and finally, as if the horrible weather, roads, and hostile local citizens were not enough, Meade ordered elements of Maj. Gen. Alfred Pleasonton's cavalry corps to pursue, harass, and capture the wagon train. As a result, numerous attacks, raids, and skirmishes ensued throughout Imboden's journey from Gettysburg to the banks of the Potomac River. Many wagons and supplies were either captured or destroyed and some of the wounded and the able-bodied Confederates accompanying them were captured. Several recent studies focus on the story of this series of engagements during Imoboden's movement toward the Potomac and should be consulted for more detail about this phase of the Gettysburg Campaign.

While Imboden led his wagon train toward Virginia, both Lee and Meade were busy in Gettysburg. Once Lee was convinced Meade would not promptly follow up on the slaughter of July 3 with an offensive movement, he issued orders to his army for an orderly withdrawal of all remaining troops from Pennsylvania, with the exception of those who were severely wounded. Lee's officers and men who were too critically wounded to be moved and a small contingent of the Army of Northern Virginia's medical personnel to care for them would remain behind. In his usual methodical way, Lee kept Confederate States of America president Jefferson Davis in Richmond informed about his plans. While his army had been ravaged by casualties during the three days of battles in and around Gettysburg, they had gained valuable provisions and other supplies, captured enemy soldiers, gathered intelligence, and had drawn the Army of the Potomac from Virginia. The latter enabled Virginia families tend to their crops more or less unmolested by Union troops.

Meade, keeping his men in their July 3 positions, began the grim task of gathering and burying the dead. His surgeons tended to the wounded while he provided frequent updates to the War Department. The U. S. Army's General-in-Chief, Henry W. Halleck, and President Lincoln were provided a fairly up-to-date and detailed picture of Meade's dispositions. What the president could not comprehend was why Meade did not act on the opportunity to follow up his July 3 victory with a crushing blow to Lee's army. Rather, Meade requested more men and supplies. Lincoln's euphoria of July 4 turned into frustration with Meade's lack of quick and aggressive action, beyond deploying Pleasonton's cavalry to harass Imboden's rebel wagon train.

During the period of July 4 through 13 Lee and then Meade led their armies away from Gettysburg and toward the Potomac crossing at Williamsport, Maryland. For the Army of Northern Virginia, the Potomac stood between them and their namesake state (newly designated *West* Virginia). Lee ordered his army to move via a different route to the Potomac River than that selected for Imboden and his wagons. Imboden's route went west from Gettysburg and then south through Greencastle and on to Williamsport. As noted previously, Imboden and his wagon train were constantly attacked by Federal cavalry during their trek southward. Following their arrival at Williamsport, Imboden's command of cavalrymen, teamsters, and the wounded faced multiple frontal attacks by the horsemen from Brig. Gen. John Buford's First Division cavalry on the afternoon and evening of July 6. The main force of Lee's army followed a more southern route that took them through Fairfield, Monterey Pass, and then to Hagerstown, just northeast of the Williamsport Potomac crossing. By the evening of July 6 the main body of the Army of Northern Virginia, led by Longstreet's corps, began to arrive at Hagerstown. The march had been challenging due to the combination of rain, bad roads, harassing Federal cavalry, and the burden of captured provisions and other supplies. In spite of these factors, the army's movement was both orderly and disciplined.

Once Lee's men reached Williamsport, they found the Potomac River was at flood level due to the heavy summer rains. As such, it could not be forded by men, horses, or rolling stock. Their lightly guarded pontoon bridge several miles down river at Falling Waters, which had been used during the advance into Pennsylvania, had been captured and destroyed by a small Federal cavalry patrol on July 4. Another pontoon bridge had to be constructed and installed. Unable to ford the swollen river and without a pontoon bridge, a small ferry at Williamsport, which followed a cable across the river, had to be used in the interim to slowly shuttle both men and supplies back and forth across. Unhappily, Lee found his army trapped in Maryland, forced to wait for the river to recede. He ordered his engineers to reconstruct the pontoon bridge at Falling Waters.

The engineers were also ordered to design, and Lee's troops to build, extensive defensive fortifications around Hagerstown and Williamsport. Entrenchments and gun emplacements were constructed along the entire line occupied by Lee's army over the next several days. Lee well understood and demanded the advantage of strong field fortifications to enhance the already strong defensive positions of his entire force. As long as their backs were to the brown rushing waters of the Potomac, the army would remain entrenched behind tons of Maryland earth, lumber, and stone. And all the time, eyes were on the river, watching for signs the water was receding.

Apart from Pleasonton's cavalry, Meade's army still remained in and around Gettysburg.

Meade's requests to Washington for more men and supplies continued. By the afternoon of July 6, Meade's troops had begun their movement from Gettysburg through Pennsylvania toward Maryland and the Potomac River. Meanwhile, President Lincoln read the incoming telegrams at the War Department closely and grew increasingly frustrated with the seemingly slow pursuit by Meade's army. From Lincoln's perspective, this was an opportunity to close on Lee's trapped army and crush it. He believed he only had to prod Meade to strike the blow which, perhaps, could serve to end the bloody conflict. It must be noted though, Meade remained under orders to keep his army between Lee's force and Washington in addition to the push to pursue and engage his foe before they crossed the Potomac.

Over the next week, Lee's men were busy with a variety of critical activities. The surgeons tended to the wounded in Hagerstown and Williamsport. Public and private buildings were transformed into hospitals. Local citizens were pressed into service feeding, clothing, and tending to the wounded and others occupying the area. Wounded, who could be moved, were shuttled across the Potomac at Williamsport into Virginia by way of the ferry. Prisoners were ferried across into Virginia and much needed supplies and ammunition for the army in Maryland arrived with each return trip.

The roads beyond Williamsport and Hagerstown were covered by cavalry patrols and pickets constantly scanning for any sign of Meade's main force. Lee's men continued to deal daily with the aggressive presence of the Federal cavalry.

By July 8, Meade's army neared Lee's force from the southeast by way of three passes in the mountains (Turner's, Fox's, and Crampton's), through the town of Middletown and toward Boonsboro which was already occupied by

Federal cavalry under Buford and Third Division commander Brig. Gen. Judson Kilpatrick.

By July 11, Meade's entire force surrounded Lee's army. The Federal troops stretched from north of Funkstown to beyond Jones Crossroads. Now nearly parallel to Meade, Lee's army extended from north of Hagerstown to beyond Downsville, located to the south. During this period, the probes and advances by Federal cavalry triggered engagements with Lee's army at Williamsport, Hagerstown, Funkstown, and Boonsboro. The newspapers throughout the north wrote with anticipation about a "second battle of Antietam" both due to the proximity to the Sharpsburg battlefield and the potential for another tremendous clash between the armies.

In spite of a series of telegraphed orders and related messages from the War Department in Washington, Meade delayed any significant general action against Lee's trapped army. On the evening of July 12, similar to July 2 at Gettysburg, Meade called his commanders for another Council of War. Several of Meade's most experience senior officers had been killed or wounded at Gettysburg. Less seasoned commanders now filled those roles. Meade included his new chief of staff, Maj. Gen. Andrew A. (A. A.) Humpreys, Maj. Gen. Gouveneur K. Warren, the chief engineer of the Army of the Potomac, Pleasonton, and seven corps commanders. The majority decision of the field commanders (staff officers did not qualify to vote on such decisions) was to only probe the enemy lines on July 13. This was to be followed by a reconnaissance in force beginning at dawn on July 14. In the interim, Meade's troops would continue to entrench opposite the length of Lee's lines.

Lee, who was quite knowledgeable about rivers from his assignments over many years as an engineer with the U. S. Army (in particular his work on the Mississippi River), closely monitored the depth and current of the Potomac River. It was determined the depth of the river was decreasing. At the same time Meade's army now opposed the entire length of Lee's lines outside of Williamsport. The Army of Northern Virginia's supplies of flour and forage in Maryland dwindled. Lee impatiently inquired as to when his engineers would complete the reconstruction of the pontoon bridge at the Falling Waters crossing. Although his army was now entrenched in strong defensive positions and munitions had been shuttled back to his army on the return trips on the rafts crossing at Williamsport, remaining any longer in Maryland did not support Lee's strategic objectives. It was time to return to Virginia. Orders were written, issued, and then communicated to Lee's commanders. The army would begin its movement from Maryland back into Virginia.

Meade's consolidated force was finally in position to attack Lee's entrenched army before it could cross the river. Military and civilian officials in Washington and Richmond, the citizens supporting the north and the south, and even foreign leaders and journalists, focused on events in the little western Maryland canal town of Williamsport.

Related Reports by the Commanding Generals

Army of Northern Virginia

Lee wrote in his official report of the Gettysburg Campaign about the period from just following the final engagement in Pennsylvania through the period just before the crossing of the Potomac River by his army:

"Owing to the strength of the enemy's position, and the reduction of our ammunition, a renewal of the engagement could not be hazarded, and the difficulty of procuring supplies rendered it impossible to continue longer where we were. Such of the wounded as were in condition to be removed, and part of the arms collected on the field, were ordered to Williamsport.

"The army remained at Gettysburg during the 4th, and at night began to retire by the road to Fairfield, carrying with it about 4,000 prisoners. Nearly 2,000 had previously been paroled, but the enemy's numerous wounded that had fallen into our hands after the first and second days' engagements were left behind.

"Little progress was made that night, owing to a severe storm, which greatly embarrassed our movements. The rear of the column did not leave its position near Gettysburg until after daylight on the 5th. The march was continued during that day without interruption from the enemy, excepting an unimportant demonstration upon our rear in the afternoon when near Fairfield, which was easily checked. Part of our train moved by the road through Fairfield and the rest by way of Cashtown, guarded by General Imboden. In passing through the mountains in advance of the column, the great length of the trains exposed them to attack by the enemy's cavalry, which captured a number of wagons and ambulances, but they succeeded in reaching Williamsport without serious loss.

"They were attacked at that place on the 6th by the enemy's cavalry, which was gallantly repulsed by General Imboden. The attacking force was subsequently encountered and driven off by General Stuart, and pursued for several miles in the direction of Boonsborough. The army, after an arduous march, rendered more difficult by the rains, reached Hagerstown on the afternoon of July 6 and morning of the 7th.

"The Potomac was found to be so much swollen by the rains that had fallen almost incessantly since our entrance into Maryland as to be un-fordable. Our communications with the south side were thus interrupt-ed, and it was difficult to procure either ammunition or subsistence, the latter difficulty being enhanced by the high waters impeding the work-ing of the neighboring mills. The trains with the wounded and prisoners were compelled to await at Williamsport the subsiding of the river and the construction of boats, as the pontoon bridge left at Falling Waters had been partially destroyed. The enemy had not yet made his appear-ance, but as he was in condition to obtain large re-enforcements, and our situation, for the reasons above mentioned, was becoming daily more embarrassing, it was deemed advisable to recross the river. Part of the pontoon bridge was recovered and new boats built, so that by the 13th a good bridge was thrown over the river at Falling Waters.

"The enemy in force reached our front on the 12th. A position had been previously selected to cover the Potomac from Williamsport to Falling Waters, and an attack was awaited during that and the succeeding day. This did not take place, though the two armies were in close proxim-ity, the enemy being occupied in fortifying his own lines."

Army of the Potomac

Meade, as commander of the Army of the Potomac, documented at a fairly high level the movements and actions of his force from July 4 through July 12 in his official report:

"On the morning of the 4th, reconnaissances developed that the enemy had drawn back his left flank, but maintained his position in front of our left, apparently assuming a new line parallel to the mountains.

"On the morning of the 5th, it was ascertained the enemy was in full retreat by the Fairfield and Cashtown roads. The Sixth Corps was immediately sent in pursuit on the Fairfield road, and the cavalry on the Cashtown road and by the Emmitsburg and Monterey Passes.

"July 5 and 6 were employed in succoring the wounded and burying the dead. Major-General Sedgwick, commanding the Sixth Corps, having pushed the pursuit of the enemy as far as the Fairfield Pass, in the mountains, and reporting that the pass was a very strong one, in which a small force of the enemy could hold in check and delay for a considerable time any pursuing force, I determined to follow the enemy by a flank movement, and, accordingly, leaving McIntosh's brigade of cavalry and Neill's brigade of infantry to continue harassing the enemy, put the army in motion for Middletown, Md. Orders were immediately sent to Major-General French at Frederick to reoccupy Harper's Ferry and send a force to occupy Turner's Pass, in South Mountain. I subsequently ascertained Major-General French had not only anticipated these orders in part, but had pushed a cavalry force to Williamsport and Falling Waters, where they destroyed the enemy's pontoon bridge and captured its guard. Buford was at the same time sent to Williamsport and Hagerstown.

"The duty above assigned to the cavalry was most successfully accomplished, the enemy being greatly harassed, his trains destroyed, and many captures of guns and prisoners made.

"After halting a day at Middletown to procure necessary supplies and bring up the trains, the army moved through the South Mountain, and by July 12 was in front of the enemy, who occupied a strong position on the heights of Marsh Run, in advance of Williamsport. In taking this position, several skirmishes and affairs had been had with the enemy, principally by the cavalry and the Eleventh and Sixth Corps."

Chapter 2

July 13

Lee Crosses the Potomac into Virginia as Meade Prepares to Attack

Monday, July 13, was filled with intense activity for Lee's Army of Northern Virginia after days of digging and waiting. Lee's orders to leave the entrenchments and cross the Potomac River under the cover of night were communicated throughout the command. Maj. Gen. James Ewell Brown "Jeb" Stuart was ordered to have his dismounted troopers fill the places left by the infantrymen in the entrenchments.

The Army of Northern Virginia's infantry waited in their positions until dusk. It rained the entire day and by evening it was raining heavily, accompanied by lightning and thunder. Through the driving rain the march down muddy back roads began. It was like that from Gettysburg—but this time the rain and the lightning were even worse.

Lieut. Gen. Richard S. Ewell and his Second Corps traveled from just southwest of Hagerstown to and through the town of Williamsport to a ford north of where Conococheague Creek feeds into the Potomac River. They had to scramble across the slippery earthen ramps that had been constructed by Lee's engineers and pioneers over the near side of the C&O Canal, and then they moved over the canal itself and down a steep incline into the still deep and dark waters of the Potomac. Torches alone lit the way for the soaked, muddy, and mostly barefoot men. Some men removed their trousers and those who had shoes and socks removed them, too. All took off their leather and tarred canvas accouterments. As they slid, stumbled, and shuffle-stepped into the river waters, they held whatever they did not want to be immersed (even though they were already soaked from the rain) over their heads—including their arms and ammunition. While not as swift as it had been only days earlier, the current of the Potomac still rushed against the crossing soldiers, wagons, horses, and mules. Once they reached the other side of the river, they had to scramble up another earthen and timber ramp that had been constructed on the far bank and continue the march away from the crossing point to their designated bivouac areas. Torches flickered, the orders barked by both commissioned officers and noncommissioned officers cut through the sounds of the pelting rain and the accompanying thunder.

Ewell's wagons and artillery were ordered to move through Williamsport. Some of the wagons had crossed by ferry prior to the foot soldiers. Still other wagons forded the Potomac. Much of the wagon train and most of Ewell's artillery followed along the C&O Canal towpath southward as it hugged the river. Nearly ten miles down river they would cross over the new pontoon bridge at Falling Waters rather than risk fording the still deep river at Williamsport. In the darkness and rain, the horses, mules, and oxen, weak from lack of forage, slowly pulled the wagons, ammunition, and guns from in and around the trenches and the town, down the narrow and now slick towpath toward the Falling Waters crossing. The darkness was only relieved by the occasional torch and the flashes of lightning. The curses of the teamsters and gunners combined with the rumble and cracks of the thunder during the journey toward the crossing point.

Lieut. Gen. James "Old Pete" Longstreet and his First Corps and Lieut. Gen. Ambrose Powell "A. P." Hill and his Third Corps followed their orders to move from their entrenchments south of Ewell's position toward a peninsula of land with a narrow road running down the center of it—Falling Waters Road. Hill's forces evacuated their positions east of Williamsport. Longstreet's men abandoned their entrenchments southeast of Williamsport, south of Hill's men and reaching to somewhat beyond the tiny hamlet of Downsville. The single country road running the length of the finger of rolling land approached the newly rebuilt pontoon bridge at a crossing known as Falling Waters for a small waterfall on the Virginia side of the river. As the men from both Longstreet's and Hill's corps marched toward Falling Waters, Stuart's cavalrymen dismounted and took their designated positions in the now empty earthworks—although at exceedingly open intervals. Campfires had been left burning by the departing troops and they continued to burn into the night.

Wagons, caissons, and guns from Lee's three corps clattered across the pontoon bridge at Falling Waters. Behind them, the lean veterans from Longstreet's corps moved down the quagmire of Falling Waters Road. No doubt some remarks were exchanged between soldiers about seeing each other back on Confederate soil. Both Longstreet's and Hill's corps had the relative luxury of a pontoon bridge crossing unlike their comrades in Ewell's corps who had orders to ford the river. But first they had to reach that river—no easy task given the conditions. Each step in the mud and rain was a struggle for the hungry and exhausted men. Those who still had shoes, found them sucked off their feet by the mud. Those too tired, hungry, or weak to continue the slog fell to the rear of their units. Ultimately, many of the exhausted stragglers simply dropped along either side of Falling Waters Road or into the farmers' fields on both sides of the road.

Throughout the night and into the early morning of July 14, both Longstreet's and Hill's men continued their journey toward and then down the length of Falling Waters Road. Longstreet's command was in the lead, followed by Hill's men. The wagons of the Army of Northern Virginia that had not been floated across the river on ferries or forded at Williamsport crossed the Potomac at Falling Waters. All the precious artillery including the guns, limbers, and other horse drawn support, also had to cross the pontoon bridge. As Longstreet's soldiers arrived toward the end of Falling Waters Road and near the pontoon bridge they received their orders to wait. The wagons and artillery had to cross the river first. They waited in the rain by torchlight for orders to cross over the C&O Canal, down to the river, and across the newly reconstructed pontoon bridge into Virginia.

Hill was ordered to provide a rear guard to cover the movement across the Potomac at Falling Waters. He assigned this duty to Maj. Gen. Henry "Harry" Heth who commanded a division within his corps and had been slightly wounded in the fighting at Gettysburg. As such, Heth's men would cover the rear of the troop movement and be among the last—with the exception of the cavalry troopers under "Jeb" Stuart—to leave Maryland. Heth and those in his command accepted serving as the rear of the long column of soaked, muddy men in gray and butternut as an honor. The word had been passed through the chain of command that a screen of Stuart's horsemen remained between them and any advancing Yankee soldiers.

Lee personally supervised his men and materiel crossing the Potomac. As July 13 ended and July 14 began, Lee and his officers grew increasingly distressed at how the weather and the condition of the roads were slowing the pace of the crossings. They were behind schedule and surely daylight would bring Meade's men in force. The entire Army of Northern Virginia—including Stuart's cavalry—was to be across the river before first light on July 14. But Longstreet's men backed up near the Maryland side of the pontoon bridge crossing and, in turn, Hill's men backed up along the length of Falling Waters Road. At the tail of Hill's column, Heth's rear guard force moved toward the crest of a hill approximately two miles from the crossing. Here they would occupy excellent defensive positions selected by Lee's engineers and constructed by the army's pioneers. Heth's men were to hold these positions until ordered to cross into Virginia and then to relinquish their positions to the horsemen under Stuart.

July 13 found Meade's Army of the Potomac entrenched opposite and parallel to the lines of the Army of Northern Virginia. Meade, his commanders, other officers, and the men spent the day in preparation for an advance against Lee's positions the next day. Meade and his Chief of Staff, Humphreys, rode along the army's lines to review the positions and the terrain. It is likely, given the rolling hills of the area, they looked across to view Lee's fortifications using their field glasses. Orders were written and issued for a reconnaissance in force by Meade's force on July 14. The action was to begin at 7:00 A.M.

Telegraph communications linked Meade's headquarters and those of his subordinate commanders. Meade desired to have the ability to both give orders and also to receive reports from his field commanders once the enemy was engaged.

Probes by both Union infantry and cavalry occurred early in the day on July 13, but no significant attacks from Meade's force pressed Lee's positions that day. The most aggressive action was taken by the Army of the Potomac's cavalry. Kilpatrick and his troopers were situated on the far right of Meade's lines near Hagerstown. Buford and his cavalry were positioned on the far left of Meade's line near Downsville. With Kilpatrick was newly promoted Brig. Gen. George Armstrong Custer commanding the 2[d] Brigade, 3[d] Division, Cavalry Corps— the Michigan Wolverines. Custer noted in his report his men actively engaged in skirmishing on July 13 and this fighting resulted in three casualties.

Otherwise, July 13 continued to be spent doing the things soldiers do before battle: they continued to dig entrenchments, officers passed orders down the chain of command and wrote their reports, and soldiers wrote home and prepared their weapons and other equipment for the upcoming fight. Although actively engaged in skirmishes with the rebels, Meade's horsemen, when not actually fighting, continued the endless routine of feeding, watering and grooming their mounts.

The Army of the Potomac prepared for battle. July 14 would be Meade's day, just as July 3 had been in Pennsylvania. Although his cavalry had been actively and aggressively engaging Lee's army nonstop since July 4, the rest of Meade's force had remained relatively unscathed since "Pickett's Charge" at Gettysburg. Meade's army was now parallel to that of Lee which was completely entrenched and with their gray backs to the still swollen river. Meade recognized it could become a major battle and the victor of Gettysburg had witnessed the effect constant musketry and artillery fire could have on an advancing force the previous December at Fredericksburg. The Federal casualties had been appalling. Any attack on Lee's fortifications which guarded the river crossings at and south of Williamsport had the potential for being every bit as bloody for the officers and men under his new command.

Official Reports and First-Hand Accounts

Army of Northern Virginia

Gen. Robert E. Lee (from his official report):
"Our preparations being completed, and the river, though still deep, being pronounced fordable, the army commenced to withdraw to the south side on the night of the 13th. Ewell's corps forded the river at Williamsport."

Lieut. Col. Walter H. Taylor, Lee's Adjutant General, later recorded:
"What a night it was! The rain was again coming down in torrents; the mud was frightful, making the movements of the artillery, ammunition-wagons, and ambulances very slow, and so retarding the movements of the troops." (Walter H. Taylor, *General Lee, His Campaigns in Virginia, 1861–1865*, p. 213)

Lieut. Gen. Ambrose P. Hill (from his official report):

"At Hagerstown, we lay in line of battle from the 7th to the night of the 13th, when I moved my corps in the direction of the pontoon bridge at Falling Waters."

Maj. Gen. Henry Heth (from his supplementary report):

"I have the honor to submit the following report of the operations of my command (Heth's and Pender's Divisions) at Falling Waters, July 14:

"On the evening of July 13, I received orders to withdraw my command at dark from the intrenchments near Hagerstown, and move in the direction of Falling Waters, at which point we were to cross the river on a pontoon bridge, already constructed. The artillery attached to my command received its orders through its immediate commander, and moved off a little before dark. I was directed to leave the skirmishers in my front, and was informed that they would be relieved during the night by the cavalry. The officers in charge of the skirmishers were directed, as soon as relieved, to take the road followed by the divisions.

"The night was entirely dark and the roads in a dreadful condition, the entire distance between our breastworks and Falling Waters being ankle-deep in mud. The progress of the command was necessarily very slow and tedious, halting every few minutes to allow the wagons and artillery in our front to pass on. The division was twelve hours accomplishing 7 miles, once halting for two hours."

Lieut. Col. S. G. Shepard, 7th Tennessee Infantry, Archer's brigade (from his report):

"We next took position between Hagerstown and Williamsport, where we lay in line of battle two days, and retired on the night of the 13th instant. Owing to the darkness of the night and the impossibility of the artillery getting on, we found ourselves 5 miles from the river at daylight."

Lieut. Col. John J. Garnett, C. S. Army, commanding Artillery Battalion, Third Corps (from his report):

"On reaching Hagerstown, the battalion was reunited under Major Richardson, who continued in command until the morning of the day on which the army fell back across the Potomac, when I resumed the command.

"I regret to state that, owing to the jaded condition of the horses, which had been but scantily supplied with forage since July 1, during all of which time they had not received a single feed of corn, I was forced to abandon two rifled pieces belonging to Captain [J. W.] Lewis' battery on the night of the retreat from Maryland. Every effort was made to bring them off, but being the rear of the artillery, and before my arrangements could be completed, which were made with all possible dispatch, the enemy's cavalry charged and took them, together with 6 men and spare horses which had been sent back for the purpose of bringing them off."

Brig. Gen. James H. Lane, C. S. Army, commanding a brigade (from his report):

"On the 13th, we lost 1 man killed in the works and had 27 skirmishers captured. The skirmishers were taken by a body of the enemy that advanced from a point of woods under cover of stone fences and an orchard.

"The retreat from Hagerstown the night of the 13th was even worse than that from Gettysburg."

Col. William L. J. Lowrance, 34th North Carolina Infantry, commanding Scales' brigade (from his report):

"We remained in line of battle near this place until the evening of the 4th, when we retreated to Hagerstown, where we arrived on the 7th and remained until the 11th, and were then drawn out in line of battle, and remained so until the night of the 13th, during which time the enemy were drawn up in our front, but remained inactive, excepting some skirmishing, which resulted in loss on our part of 2 killed, several wounded, and several captured."

Jedediah Hotchkiss, the topographer for Ewell's Second Corps, who kept a detailed journal during the campaign, recorded on July 13:

"We were up and breakfasted at an early hour, about 4 A.M., the skirmishing beginning about that time, and all thought we would surely have a desperate battle, but the firing soon ceased and comparative quiet reigned along the lines most of the day. There was a gradual movement of our forces to the right as the enemy was concentrating in that direction. Yesterday our Engineer troops made boats to supply the place of those we had lost, and today, by noon, the pontoon was finished at Falling Waters and the river became fordable at Williamsport, so we passed our wagons over rapidly. I went down and saw my wagon safely ferried over—then came back to our headquarters on the Williamsport Road, then went along down our line and passed over the pontoon at Falling Waters. Our wagons soon came up and I went with the men to Camp Stevens, four and a half miles from Martinsburg. The train passed the pontoon quite rapidly; the artillery began to move about dark, the infantry also began to move towards the river—the cavalry taking their places along the lines. It rained throughout the day and very hard at night; all were very weary; it was quite late when we encamped; the whole Virginia shore was alive with wagons." (Jedediah Hotchkiss, *Make Me a Map of the Valley,* Edited by Archie P. McDonald, pp. 160–1)

Maj. Gen. J. E. B. Stuart (from his report):
"The 13th was spent in reconnoitering on the left, Rodes' division occupying the extreme left of our infantry, very near Hagerstown, a little north of the National road. Cavalry pickets were extended beyond the railroad leading to Chambersburg, and everything put in readiness to resist the enemy's attack. The situation of our communications south of the Potomac caused the commanding general to desire more cavalry on that side, and, accordingly, Brigadier-General Jones' brigade (one of whose regiments, Twelfth Virginia Cavalry, had been left in Jefferson) was detached, and sent to cover our communication with Winchester. The cavalry on the left consisted now of Fitz. Lee's, W. H. F. Lee's, Baker's, and Robertson's brigades, the latter being a mere handful.

"On the 13th, skirmishing continued at intervals, but it appeared that the enemy, instead of attacking, was intrenching himself in our front, and the commanding general determined to cross the Potomac. The night of the 13th was chosen for this move, and the arduous and difficult task of bringing up the rear was, as usual, assigned to the cavalry. Just before night (which was unusually rainy), the cavalry was disposed from right to left, to occupy, dismounted, the trenches of the infantry at dark, Fitz. Lee's brigade holding the line of Longstreet's corps, Baker's of Hill's corps, and the remainder of Ewell's corps. A pontoon bridge had been constructed at Falling Waters, some miles below Williamsport, where Longstreet's and Hill's corps were to cross, and Ewell's corps was to ford the river at Williamsport, in rear of which last, after daylight, the cavalry was also to cross, excepting that Fitz. Lee's brigade, should he find the pontoon bridge clear in time, was to cross at the bridge; otherwise to cross at the ford at Williamsport.

"The operation was successfully performed by the cavalry. General Fitz. Lee, finding the bridge would not be clear in time for his command, moved after daylight to the ford, sending two squadrons to cross in rear of the infantry at the bridge. These squadrons, mistaking Longstreet's rear for the rear of the army on that route, crossed over in rear of it."

Lieut. Col. W. W. Blackford, who served as "Jeb" Stuart's Adjutant, later recorded:

"On the night of the 13th, orders were issued for the crossing, the infantry drawing out of the entrenchments and the cavalry taking their places; then as soon as the infantry had crossed the cavalry followed. Longstreet's and Hill's corps crossed on pontoon bridges, which had been rebuilt, at Falling Waters, while Ewell's corps forded at Williamsport and the cavalry all forded at Williamsport also. The ford was very wide and still almost past fording. I witnessed the passage of Ewell's corps and it was a strange and interesting sight. On either bank fires illuminated the scene, the water reached the armpits of the men and was very swift. By the bright lurid light the long line of heads and musket barrels could be traced across the watery space, dwindling away almost to a thread before it reached the further shore. The passage of the wagon trains was attended with some loss, for the current in some cases swept them down past the ford into deep water. It was curious to watch the behavior of the mules in these teams. As the water rose over their backs they began rearing and springing vertically upward, and as they went deep and deeper the less would be seen of them before they made the spring which would bring their bodies half out of the water; then nothing would be seen but their ears above the water, until by a violent effort the poor brutes would again spring aloft; and indeed after the water had closed over them, occasionally one would appear in one last plunge above the surface." (Lieut. Col. W. W. Blackford, C.S.A., *War Years with Jeb Stuart,* pp. 234–5)

Lieut. William R. Carter of the 3[d] Virginia Cavalry who served under Fitzhugh Lee recorded:

"July 13: Several hundred men engaged in building a pontoon bridge at Falling Waters on the Potomac. Moved out today & went towards our left wing & then towards our right to Downsville. After dark we were ordered to re-enforce Col. Wickham & cover the retreat of our army. Gen. R. E. Lee having waited for the enemy several days & finding that they were throwing up substantial works, behind which they could retire in case of defeat, and besides, that they were indisposed to attack him, seeing too that he had exhausted his supplies in the territory then occupied, determined to recross the Potomac at Williamsport & a pontoon bridge at Falling Waters. We were ordered to put out pickets & relieve the Infantry pickets who retired at midnight. Very heavy rain tonight." (Lieut. Col. William R. Carter, *Sabres, Saddles and Spurs,* Edited by Col. Walbrook D. Swank, p. 82)

Brig. Gen. William N. Pendleton, C. S. Army, Chief of Artillery (from his report):

"In full expectation of a decisive battle here, the army was, by the commanding general, called upon for its utmost efforts, and I was specially directed to see that everything possible was accomplished by the artillery. Accordingly, for three days, during which the enemy was waited for, my best energies were given, with those of others, to the work of arrangement and preparation. The enemy, however, prudently forbore, and, it being undesirable to await him longer, our army was, on the night of the 13th, withdrawn to the south bank of the Potomac. In this movement, necessarily involving much labor, greatly increased difficulty was imposed upon those responsible for artillery operations by the enfeebled condition of horses drawing through roads saturated with rain, and by the swollen state of the river, which confined the whole army, train and all to one route across the pontoon bridge at Falling Waters. Still, the task was cheerfully undertaken, and in the main successfully accomplished."

Artillerist Col. Edward Porter Alexander recorded in his memoirs that:
"On the 13ᵗʰ, both his (Lee's) bridge and the ford near Williamsport were passable, and orders were issued to make the crossing during that night. The river had fallen to a stage barely permitting infantry to ford, but about dark it again began to rise. Ewell's corps was ordered to cross by the ford. Longstreet, followed by Hill, was to cross by the pontoon bridge. Caissons were ordered to start from the lines at 5 P.M., the infantry and artillery at dark ...

"Another rain storm had set in before dusk, and it kept up nearly all night. It was the dark period of the moon and the blackness of the night was phenomenal. The rout to the bridge was over small farm roads, rough, narrow and hilly. Already from the incessant rains they were in bad condition, and now, under the long procession of heavy wheels, churning in the mud, they became canals of slush in which many vehicles were hopelessly stalled." (Gen. Edward Porter Alexander, *Military Memoirs of a Confederate,* pp. 438–9)

Army of the Potomac

Maj. Gen. George G. Meade (from his report):
"The 13th was occupied in reconnaissances of the enemy's position and preparations for attack ..."

What Meade did not record in his official report was later captured in the biography of General-in-Chief Henry Halleck:
"On July 13, Meade informed Halleck: 'In my dispatch of yesterday I stated that it was my intention to attack the enemy to-day, unless something intervened to prevent it. Upon calling my corps commanders together and submitting the question to them, five out of six were unqualifiedly opposed to it.'"

"Old Brains" (Halleck) responded:
"You are strong enough to attack and defeat the enemy before he can affect a crossing. Act on your own judgment and make your generals execute your orders. Call no council of war. It is proverbial that council's

of war never fight. Re-enforcements are pushed on as rapidly as possible. Do no let the enemy escape." (Curt Anders, *Henry Halleck's War, A Fresh Look at Lincoln's Controversial General-in-Chief,* p. 458)

A similar tone was captured in the diary of President Abraham Lincoln's Assistant Presidential Secretary John Hay:

"The President begins to grow anxious and impatient about Meade's silence. I thought and told him there was nothing to prevent the enemy from getting away by the Falling Waters, if they were not vigorously attacked ... Nothing can save them, if Meade does his duty. I doubt him. He is an engineer." (John Hay, *Inside Lincoln's White House,* Edited by Michael Burlingame and John R. Turner Ettlinger, p. 62)

Capt. Lemuel B. Norton, Chief Signal Officer (from his report):

"On July 12, a party was sent to open a line of signals between general headquarters and the brigade of General Neill, near Leitersburg, but the attempt failed by reason of the thickness of the atmosphere. The signal telegraph wire was this day extended to General Sedgwick's new headquarters at Funkstown, and another run out between general headquarters and those of General Slocum, 2½ miles distant and near Four Corners. Both lines worked with but slight interruptions until the night of the 14th, when they were withdrawn. Flag signals were worked between the headquarters of the Fifth Corps and others in the vicinity; also between General Howard's headquarters, at Funkstown, and a station of observation in Hagerstown.

"On July 13, all signal communication previously established was still kept up. Two officers were sent to make a telescopic reconnaissance from Elk Mountain."

Lieut. Col. Elisha Hunt Rhodes recorded that:

"Line of battle near Hagerstown, Md. July 13/63—I have not changed my clothes for five weeks, but still I am happy, and we are doing good work.

"Last night we had a skirmish, the 2nd R.I. lost three men, one of them from my Co. 'B.' My poor little Company will soon be gone if we do not get recruits. We are now entrenched and are waiting for orders.

General Meade is popular with the troops as all Generals would be if they would only lead us to victory. We are expecting a fight here as Lee's Army is not far off. I do not understand our movements but suppose them to be all right. Time will show however." (*All for the Union, The Civil War Diary and Letters of Elisha Hunt Rhodes,* Edited by Robert Hunt Rhodes, p. 110)

Maj. Gen. Alfred Pleasonton (from his report):

"Until July 14, this division was posted on the right of the army. It was constantly engaged with the enemy, as was Buford's division, on the left, and Huey's brigade, of Gregg's division, in the center."

Brig. Gen. John Buford (from his report):

"July 12 and 13, remained at Bakersville, and pushed pickets to within 800 yards of the enemy's intrenchments at Downsville."

Brig. Gen. George A. Custer (from his report):

"On July 13, the regiment was on outpost duty, and engaged with the enemy most of the day. Loss, 3 men severely wounded."

Chapter 3

July 14
The Disposition of Lee's Rear Guard

Maj. Gen. Henry Heth's orders specified his division was to serve as the rear guard for Longstreet's and Hill's commands as they crossed the Potomac River by way of the reconstructed pontoon bridge at Falling Waters. Throughout the night of July 13 and into the morning hours of July 14, Heth's men struggled through the mud as they moved slowly toward and then down the length of Falling Waters Road. Ahead of them on the road were the wagons, artillery, and men of Longstreet's corps followed by more of the same from their corps (Hill's). Heavy rain, accompanied by lightning and thunder, continued throughout the night of July 13−14.

Approximately two miles from the river crossing, the soldiers in Heth's command arrived at the position designated in their orders. It was early morning. Their defensive line was bisected by Falling Waters Road. On the steep rise just to the right of the road was a farm house and barn. At the crest of the rise and approximately one hundred yards in front of the barn, Lee's engineers had specified six artillery lunettes or crescent-shaped earthworks be placed by the pioneers and soldiers. These six earthworks were designed to provide some degree of protection for artillery pieces and their gun crews, accommodating one field piece per lunette. The lunettes were not connected by trenches so there were open gaps between them. No field pieces stood behind the earthworks, the guns and their crews were already across the Potomac River by way of the pontoon bridge. Only two guns remained on the Maryland side of the river and these had been lost to the mud. They were reluctantly abandoned as their teams of horses were too exhausted and starved to extract them. Experienced artillery crews would have "spiked" or otherwise disabled the guns so they could not be used when captured by the enemy.

The farm house, just to the right of the road as moving toward the river, sat atop a hill. It was a rather formal, yet dilapidated, looking two story red brick Federal-style house. The front of the house faced and was only slightly set back from Falling Waters Road. To the rear of the house was a plank fence which surrounded a garden and several large trees. Unknown to the exhausted Confederates, the house had been built by a successful Irish-born Roman Catholic lawyer by the name of Daniel Donnelly. Lawyer, politician, business speculator, and militia officer, he had built the house prior in 1833. He also owned the surrounding land. A large western Maryland German-style barn constructed of wide wooden planks with a stone foundation stood to the right rear of the house. The barn had an earthen ramp on the far side. The house had not only served as home to Donnelly, his wife, children, and servants, but also as his law office. Donnelly's talent for the law and politics apparently did not translate into financial success. He invested in the C&O Canal which followed the Potomac to the rear of his land (he in fact sold some of his land to the C&O Canal Company). Speculative ventures led to his financial ruin by 1845. Donnelly's house and its contents were sold at auction in 1852. Donnelly died in 1858 and was given the honors due an officer of the Maryland Militia. He was buried in the nearby Williamsport cemetery which is nearly ten miles upstream and overlooks the Potomac. By July 1863, the only reminders of Donnelly's fleeting fame were his headstone and the grand, but somewhat neglected looking brick house and large barn. During the war, Donnelly's former house was owned by William B. McAtee who bought it along with $420^{3}/_{4}$ acres in 1852.

Heth and his staff established their headquarters at the Donnelly house. He ordered his commanders from right to left form a line of battle running across nearly the entire width of the peninsula and perpendicular to the road. To the far left of Heth's headquarters flowed the Potomac and then the C&O Canal. Cliffs with tangled thick vines grew between the canal and the rolling farmland above. To the right of the cliffs were thick woods and then farmland that ran along the ridge toward the Donnelly house. Behind the Donnelly barn and to the rear of Heth's headquarters the land dropped off into a small ravine and then continued to rise and fall the distance to the crossing at the end of the road. Just to the right of the front of the Donnelly house was Falling Waters Road. The road and the fields beyond dropped to a lower elevation than the crest on which the Donnelly house sat. The land to the right of the road gradually undulated and dropped from fields toward woods and then out of sight over a mile beyond where the C&O Canal and the river flowed after having rounded the tip of Falling Waters crossing.

The men of Heth's command, having reached the designated rear guard position nearly two miles from the pontoon crossing, moved by brigade and regiment into their now familiar line of battle. To the far left of the line was Brig. Gen. James Johnson Pettigrew's North Carolina, or First, Brigade. Pettigrew, a University of North Carolina graduate was by profession a professor, lawyer, and author. In the mid-twentieth century, he would have been referred to as a "whiz kid." Pettigrew had just turned thirty-five years old on July 4. He led Heth's Division on July 3 at Gettysburg due to the head wound its commander had suffered. Earlier in the war, Pettigrew had the misfortune of being wounded and then captured. He was exchanged after several months. Pettigrew suffered from a painful wound to his right hand as a result of the recent fighting at Gettysburg and this was in addition to his still weak left arm which had been wounded the prior year. Pettigrew's brigade included the 11th North Carolina, 26th North Carolina, 47th North Carolina, and 52d North Carolina.

To the right of Pettigrew's brigade and to the left of Falling Waters Road (and thus the center of the rear guard's line) was Archer's Third Brigade. Brig. Gen. James Jay Archer had been captured at Gettysburg and his brigade was now under the command of Lieut. Col. S. G. Shepard. Archer's brigade was comprised of the 13th Alabama, 5th Alabama Battalion, 1st Tennessee (Provisional Army), 7th Tennessee, and 14th Tennessee. At the crest of the ridge behind the Donnelly house and in front of the farm's barn, the Alabama and Tennessee men reached their line of battle positions, stacked arms, and lay down on the wet ground in their much diminished company clusters to catch a brief nap following their exhausting night march.

Below the ridge and on the right of Falling Waters Road the land slopes down into open and expansive fields. Here the command of Col. J. M. Brockenbrough's Virginians, also known as Heth's Second Brigade, formed their portion of the rear guard's line of battle. While they did not have the advantage of either a ridge or lunettes for their defensive position, they did have an excellent view

of the only road to their front because of the open fields and relatively flat terrain. Brockenbrough's command included the 40th Virginia, 47th Virginia, 55th
Virginia, and 22d Virginia Battalion. The Virginia men were undoubtedly looking
forward to crossing the Potomac into their home state.

Beyond Brockenbrough's Brigade, the line of battle continued, stretching
toward the other side of the Falling Waters peninsula in the direction of the continuing C&O Canal and Potomac. The far right of the line of battle was held by
thirty-eight-year-old Brig. Gen. Joseph R. Davis' Fourth Brigade. A Mississippi
lawyer and politician, Davis was the nephew of former U.S. Secretary of War
and now Confederate States of America President Jefferson Davis. His command
consisted of the 2d Mississippi, 11th Mississippi, 42d Mississippi, and 55th North
Carolina. Similar to the other brigades, Davis' command reached their designated positions after the difficult march from their trenches. Davis' men were
wet, muddy, hungry, and exhausted. Upon reaching their rear guard positions,
they dropped in place for a well deserved rest while they too waited for orders
to cross the Potomac into Virginia.

Along the entire line of battle straddling both sides of Falling Waters Road,
Heth, his brigade commanders, and their officers knew from their orders the
same gray-clad horsemen who had manned their earthworks the previous day
were now serving as a screen between their positions and Meade's troops.
The reality of the situation was after not being needed to hold off an attack by
the Federals, Stuart's cavalrymen evacuated the trenches. Unknown to Heth,
Pettigrew, and their staffs, twenty-eight-year-old Brig. Gen. Fitzhugh Lee, who
commanded a cavalry brigade, had somehow mistaken the rear of Longstreet's
column for Heth and his rear guard. Fitz Lee's brigade consisted of the 1st
Maryland Battalion, 1st, 2d, 3d, 4th, and 5th Virginia Cavalry. Robert E. Lee's
nephew, another graduate of the Military Academy at West Point, and his men
prepared to cross the Potomac on the Falling Waters pontoon bridge. Finding
the bridge clogged with materiel and men and falling behind the timetable, they
continued up the river to the Williamsport crossing. There the horsemen forded
the lower but still rushing river back into Virginia.

Maj. Gen. William D. Pender's Division, under the command of twenty-
nine-year-old Virginia Military Institute graduate Brig. Gen. James H. Lane,
was located between Heth's rear guard location straddling Falling Waters Road
and the pontoon bridge river crossing. On the morning of July 14, Lane's men
waited to cross into Virginia. His command consisted of four brigades. The

First Brigade was commanded by Col. Abner Perrin and included the 1ˢᵗ South Carolina (Provisional Army), 1ˢᵗ South Carolina Rifles, 12ᵗʰ, 13ᵗʰ, and 14ᵗʰ South Carolina. Lane's Second Brigade, which was his regular command, was under the leadership of Col. C. M. Avery. The Second Brigade consisted of the 7ᵗʰ, 18ᵗʰ, 28ᵗʰ, 33ᵈ, and 37ᵗʰ North Carolina. Brig. Gen. Edward L. Thomas commanded the Third Brigade. It included the 14ᵗʰ, 35ᵗʰ, 45ᵗʰ, and 49ᵗʰ Georgia. The Fourth Brigade was Brig. Gen. A. M. Scales' brigade. It was led by Col. William L. J. Lowrance. His command was composed of the 13ᵗʰ, 16ᵗʰ, 22ᵈ, 34ᵗʰ, and 38ᵗʰ North Carolina. The men of Lane's command, as wet, muddy, hungry, and bone tired as those on either side of Falling Waters Road with Heth, completed their march from the entrenchments to the river crossing and they waited for orders to walk (not march) across the pontoon bridge over the Potomac and back into Virginia.

Heth and his staff officers near the rear of the Donnelly house had an unobstructed view of the road and the rolling farmland on either side of it. They awaited orders from Hill to withdraw from their defensive positions and move to the river crossing. Heth's brigade commanders rode slowly or walked near their men as they waited for their orders. Ahead lay less than two more miles and then the river's swift and churning waters spanned by the pontoon bridge.

Official Reports and First-Hand Accounts

Army of Northern Virginia

Gen. Robert E. Lee recorded in his official report of the campaign:
"Ewell's corps forded the river at Williamsport. Those of Longstreet and Hill crossed upon the bridge. Owing to the condition of the roads, the troops did not reach the bridge until after daylight on the 14th, and the crossing was not completed until 1 p.m., when the bridge was removed. The enemy offered no serious interruption, and the movement was attended with no loss of materiel excepting a few disabled wagons and two pieces of artillery, which the horses were unable to move through the deep mud. Before fresh horses could be sent back for them, the rear of the column had passed. During the slow and tedious march to the bridge, in the midst of a violent storm of rain, some of the men lay down by the

way to rest. Officers sent back for them failed to find many in the obscurity of the night, and these, with some stragglers, fell into the hands of the enemy."

In his report, Maj. Gen. Henry Heth noted:
"On reaching an elevated and commanding ridge of hills one mile and a half (possibly a little less) from Falling Waters, I was ordered by Lieut. Gen. A. P. Hill to put my division in line of battle on either side of the road, and, extending along the crest of this hill, facing toward Hagerstown. On the left of the road and on the crest of this hill our engineers had thrown up some half dozen epaulements for artillery, the spaces between the epaulements being open. In our front was an open space, with the view unobstructed for half to three-quarters of a mile; then came a heavy piece of timber some three-fourths of a mile in width. I was directed, at the same time that I received the order to place my division in line of battle as described, to put Pender's division in the rear of my own, in column of brigades. At this point we halted, to allow the wagons and artillery to get over the river. We remained in this position awaiting their crossing for several hours."

Lieut. Col. S. G. Shepherd in command of Archer's Third Brigade reported:
"Owing to the darkness of the night and the impossibility of the artillery getting on, we found ourselves 5 miles from the river at daylight. We moved on to within 2 miles of the river, and formed a line of battle upon the crest of a hill, to protect our rear until the artillery and the column in advance of us could cross the river."

According to Maj. J. Jones of the 26th North Carolina Infantry:
"After traveling all night in mud and rain, about 8 o'clock on the morning of the 14th we took position in a wheat-field as a portion of the rear guard, while the rest of the troops crossed the river at the pontoon bridge (about 1½ miles) at Falling Waters. The men stacked arms, and most of them were asleep, feeling perfectly secure, as our cavalry were out in front."

Brig. Gen. James H. Lane who commanded Pender's Division wrote in his report:

"My whole command was so exhausted that they all fell asleep as soon as they were halted - about a mile from the pontoon bridge at Falling Waters."

Col. William L. J. Lowrance in command of Scales' Fourth Brigade recorded: "Then commenced our retreat to Falling Waters, and we arrived there at 10 o'clock on the morning of the 14th; and, while resting for a few hours ere (sic.) we crossed, whether it was in order to cross over the wagon trains, artillery, &c., I cannot say ..."

Confederate topographer Jedediah Hotchkiss noted in his diary: "Tuesday, July 14. The infantry commenced crossing the river at 1 A.M. today—Longstreet first crossing the pontoon and A. P. Hill behind him leaving a rear guard. Ewell's corps waded the river at Williamsport, the water reaching up to the arm-pits of the men. It was said that we lost 8,000 pairs of shoes in the crossing. Everything came safely over and the cavalry crossed soon this morning." (Hotchkiss, *Make Me a Map,* p. 161)

Lee's cavalry commander, Maj. Gen. J. E. B. Stuart, noted in his report: "A pontoon bridge had been constructed at Falling Waters, some miles below Williamsport, where Longstreet's and Hill's corps were to cross, and Ewell's corps was to ford the river at Williamsport, in rear of which last, after daylight, the cavalry was also to cross, excepting that Fitz. Lee's brigade, should he find the pontoon bridge clear in time, was to cross at the bridge; otherwise to cross at the ford at Williamsport.

"The operation was successfully performed by the cavalry. General Fitz. Lee, finding the bridge would not be clear in time for his command, moved after daylight to the ford, sending two squadrons to cross in rear of the infantry at the bridge. These squadrons, mistaking Longstreet's rear for the rear of the army on that route, crossed over in rear of it."

Chief of Artillery and Headquarters Liaison Officer Brig. Gen. W. N. Pendleton wrote in his report:

"With the exception of a few caissons abandoned by some officers because teams could draw them no longer, and two guns left by those in charge for like reason, the battalions were entirely across by noon of the 14th. After crossing, Carter's guns were placed in position on the hill just below the bridge, and some of Garnett's on that just above. Lane's 20-pounder Parrotts were also posted some distance farther down, and [W. B.] Hurt's Whitworths higher up, all to repel an expected advance of the enemy."

Chapter 4

July 14

The Disposition of the Army of the Potomac

Army of the Potomac commander Meade ordered a reconnaissance in force of Lee's positions for 7 A.M. on July 14. Prior to that hour, word started to reach the Federals that Lee's army had vacated their positions overnight and were crossing the Potomac River. Before daylight on July 14, some of the Army of Northern Virginia was already across the river. Ewell's (Second Army Corps) men forded at Williamsport and Longstreet (First Army Corps) and Hill (Third Army Corps), in addition to the army's artillery, crossed over the pontoon bridge at Falling Waters. Lee ordered the extensive entrenchments which surrounded Williamsport and the crossings (from north of Hagerstown to near Sharpsburg) held by Stuart's cavalrymen as the infantry and artillery withdrew to the two Potomac River crossings. Campfires and sporadic small arms fire gave the impression the Army of Northern Virginia remained entrenched.

Brig. Gen. Horatio Gouveneur Wright, age 43, who commanded the 1st Division of Sedgwick's 6th Corps, was alerted before 7 A.M. that Lee's army was on the move and assembled troops for a pursuit. Sedgwick's corps advanced on the Confederate positions only to find them empty. Meade was notified and began the process of ordering his army to pursue Lee's force by approximately 8:30 A.M.

When Kilpatrick learned of the withdrawal of Lee's army, he ordered his horsemen to leave their encampment and rapidly advance mounted toward the Confederate's positions outside of Williamsport. Kilpatrick's command included the 1ˢᵗ Brigade under Col. Nathaniel P. Richmond. Col. Richmond had stepped into the command formerly held by Brig. Gen. Elon J. Farnsworth who had been killed in a suicidal attack ordered by Kilpatrick less than two weeks earlier at Gettysburg. Richmond commanded the 5ᵗʰ New York, 18ᵗʰ Pennsylvania, 1ˢᵗ Vermont, and 1ˢᵗ West Virginia (ten companies). The 2ᵈ Brigade was commanded by Brig. Gen. George A. Custer and included the 1ˢᵗ, 5ᵗʰ, 6ᵗʰ and 7ᵗʰ (ten companies) Michigan. Kilpatrick's troopers found only empty entrenchments. They next galloped beyond the trenches and into the town of Williamsport. There they discovered stragglers and the last of Early's command which was still fording the Potomac just above the C&O Canal aqueduct over Conococheague Creek. It appeared Kilpatrick and his horsemen were too late.

Having missed the opportunity to cut off the crossing of Ewell's corps at Williamsport, a portion of Kilpatrick's cavalrymen spurred their mounts toward the Falling Waters crossing with Custer's 6ᵗʰ Michigan in the advance. Buford, in command of the 1ˢᵗ Division of the Army of the Potomac's Cavalry Corps, and his horsemen approached from the east. Buford's 1ˢᵗ Cavalry Division was composed of the 1ˢᵗ Brigade under Col. William Gamble which included the 8ᵗʰ and 12ᵗʰ Illinois, 3ᵈ Indiana, and 8ᵗʰ New York. Buford's 2ᵈ Brigade was under the command of Col. Thomas C. Devin. It included the 6ᵗʰ and 9ᵗʰ New York, 17ᵗʰ Pennsylvania, and 3ᵈ West Virginia (two companies).

Buford communicated his planned movements to Kilpatrick with the tactical objective of cutting off the part of Lee's army which had not yet crossed at Falling Waters. Kilpatrick, coming in from the north, was to draw the attention of and hold the Confederates. Buford would come in from the east and insert his force between Lee's men and the single river crossing at the end of Falling Waters Road, thus creating a trap comprised of his horsemen and those under Kilpatrick. The plan could work but coordination and timing would be crucial. How Buford or Kilpatrick were to know when the other was in position, given they would be out of visual sight of one another, remains a mystery. Perhaps they were to communicate with bugle calls or intended to utilize mounted couriers with messages. We may never know. What we do know is in any era Kilpatrick would be considered a glory seeker. He also had a reputation for being reckless. He had no intention of waiting for Buford's arrival when a portion of Lee's army was within striking distance and his troopers had the ability to attack them.

Kilpatrick's troopers galloped down Falling Waters Road toward the river crossing. Along the route they encountered Confederate stragglers and horses, along with discarded rebel arms and equipment.

Kilpatrick's command, led by the 6th Michigan, halted and then formed near a tree line with a crop field to the front. On a rise to their front and toward the right, Kilpatrick, Custer, and their officers and men could see the two story brick Donnelly house surrounded by trees. The very top of the barn may have been visible from their position (while the Donnelly House has survived and is today on the National Register of Historic Places, the barn is no longer standing, only its earthen ramp has survived). According to their reports, the Federal horsemen also noted to the right and rear of the house were six earthworks in the form of artillery lunettes. Whether these were truly visible from the tree line or noted later is open to debate. Confederate officers, mounted and on foot, and men were visible along the length of the rise. No artillery pieces or caissons were visible. The opportunity to strike the rebels before they crossed the Potomac appeared to be Kilpatrick's good fortune, even though Buford had yet to arrive. Kilpatrick, true to his reputation, decided there was no time to waste. His lead force of troopers would immediately attack rather than wait for Buford's men to arrive from the east. Kilpatrick and his men faced the enemy now and for that reason they would attack.

Official Reports and First-Hand Accounts

Army of the Potomac

Maj. Gen. George G. Meade noted in his report:
"The 13th was occupied in reconnaissances of the enemy's position and preparations for attack, but, on advancing on the morning of the 14th, it was ascertained he had retired the night previous by a bridge at Falling Waters and the ford at Williamsport."

Brig. Gen. John Buford recorded:
"July 14, at 7 a.m., the division was ordered to advance, and at 7:30 o'clock it was discovered that the enemy had evacuated during the night. The few remaining scouts were run into the rear guard of Lee's army, which was soon

seen in front of Kilpatrick, who had advanced from the north. Kilpatrick was engaged. I sent word to him that I would put my whole force in on the enemy's rear and flank, and get possession of the road and bridge in their rear."

Brig. Gen. Judson Kilpatrick stated in his official report:
"Having been previously ordered to attack at 7 a.m., I was ready to move at once. At daylight I had reached the crest of the hills occupied by the enemy an hour before, and at a few moments before 6 o'clock General Custer drove the rear guard of the enemy into the river at Williamsport. Learning from citizens that a portion of the enemy had retreated in the direction of Falling Waters, I at once moved rapidly for that point, and came up with the rear guard of the enemy at 7:30 a.m., at a point 2 miles distant from Falling Waters. We pressed on, driving them before us, capturing many prisoners and one gun. When within a mile and a half of Falling Waters the enemy was found in large force, drawn up in line of battle, on the crest of a hill commanding the road on which I was advancing. His left was protected by earthworks, and his right extended to the woods far on my left. The enemy was, when first seen, in two lines of battle, with arms stacked."

Brig. Gen. George A. Custer's 5th Michigan Cavalry report:
July 14. Led the advance toward Williamsport, and charged into the town, meeting no considerable force ..."

Custer's Battery M, 2[d] U.S. Artillery report:
"July 14. Marched to Falling Waters, via Williamsport ..."

James Henry Avery of the 5th Michigan Cavalry wrote:
"In the early morning we were again on the Pike, leading to Williamsport, but no johnnies were found, until near the town, where their rear guard were nearly across the river. We charged into town and captured a good many of them and received the parting shorts of the enemy as they were huddled on the Virginia shore. But a few shots from Pennington sent them flying.
    "We next took up our march for Falling Waters, where we arrived in time to get a parting salute and ..." (James Henry Avery, *Under Custer's Command,* Compiled by Karla Jean Husby, Edited by Eric J. Wittenberg, p. 43)

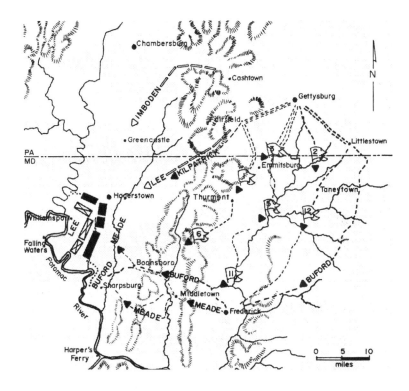

Map 1. "Chasing Lee to the Potomac" (John Heiser, *Gettysburg Magazine*, Issue Number Eleven, p. 47).

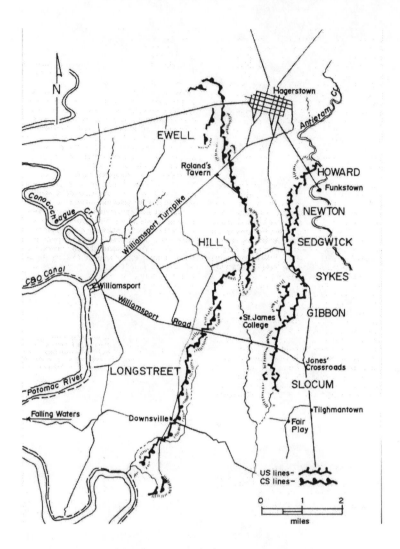

Map 2. "Position of the Armies below Hagerstown, July 13, 1863" (John Heiser, *Gettysburg Magazine*, Issue Number Twenty-Two, p. 127).

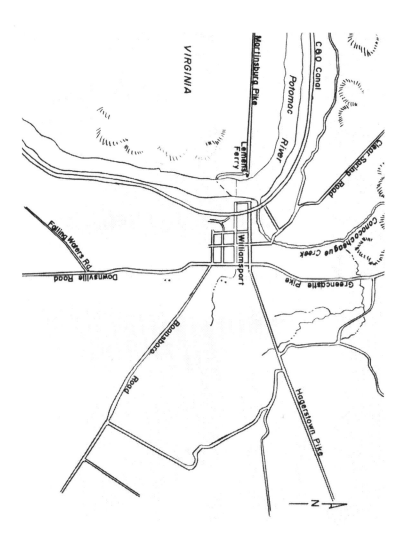

Map 3. "Williamsport and Vicinity, July 1863" (John Heiser, *Gettysburg Magazine*, Issue Number Twenty-Seven, p. 87).

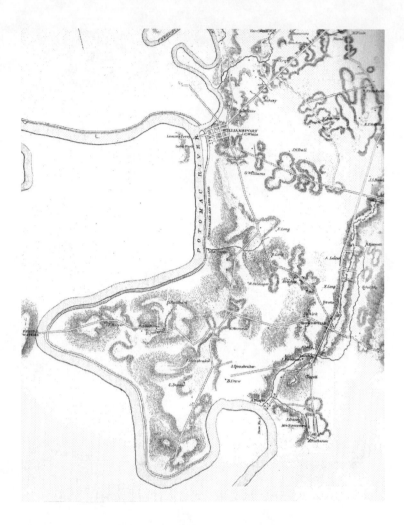

Map 4. Detail of the Falling Waters battlefield from "Map of the Vicinity of Hagerstown, Funkstown, Williamsport and Falling Waters, Md. Accompanying the Report of Major General G. G. Meade on the Battle of Gettysburg dated October 1ˢᵗ 1863" (Author's Collection).

Illustration 1. "Charge of the 6th Michigan cavalry over the rebel earthworks nr. Falling Waters," Alfred Waud, 1863 (Library of Congress).

Illustration 2. "Gallant charge by two companies of the 6th Michigan on Tuesday morning on the rebel rearguard, near Falling Waters …," Edwin Forbes, 1863 (Library of Congress).

Illustration 3. Brig. Gen. J. Johnston Pettigrew (*Confederate Military History*, 1899).

Illustration 4. Brig. Gen. George A. Custer, 1863 (Library of Congress).

Chapter 5

July 14

The Attack by Kilpatrick's Cavalry at Falling Waters

Kilpatrick's horsemen halted and briefly rested their mounts at the tree line, approximately a mile from the rebel positions. There they waited for orders after the frantic dash from Williamsport. The troopers were mud splattered as a result of the morning's race from near Hagerstown to Williamsport then to their current position.

Meanwhile, Buford and his troopers were winding their way from the east to Falling Waters, intent on cutting off the rebels in a coordinated movement with Kilpatrick before the rebels could cross into Virginia.

Heth, his brigade commanders, officers, and men rested in their new positions on the ridge behind the Donnelly house and along the battle line on both sides of and nearly perpendicular to Falling Waters Road. Those who could sleep did so, having been awake the entire night as they slogged in the rain toward the Potomac River. Now, within two miles of the river crossing, they waited to return to the road leading to the pontoon bridge and Virginia. As they waited, Heth and his officers were confident due to the assurance Stuart's cavalry remained between them and any advancing Yankee troops.

From his tree line position off the left side of Falling Waters Road, Kilpatrick was, as always, eager for a chance to engage the rebels. But Buford's troopers were nowhere to be seen. Kilpatrick was not going to let more of Lee's men escape by hesitating. It had been a long chase since leaving Gettysburg. After considering his tactical options, Kilpatrick ordered Custer to provide troopers from his Wolverines, who were in the advance of the mounted force, for an immediate assault against the rebel position on the ridge. Custer in turn ordered Maj. Peter A. Weber of the 6th Michigan Cavalry to lead the attack. Custer ordered Weber's men to advance dismounted toward the Confederate earthworks. They were armed with Spencer rifles rather than the more common carbines usually carried by Union horsemen. Custer's tactics were not in line with Kilpatrick's assessment of the situation and the overly aggressive "Kill-Cavalry" Kilpatrick countermanded Custer's orders. He instead directed Major Weber to lead approximately 100 men from Companies B and F of the 6th Michigan Cavalry in a mounted attack against the rebel earthworks on the ridge.

The fields and road to the front of Weber and his troopers were still thick with mud from heavy rains falling throughout the night. The steep hill leading to the ridge ahead was certain to challenge the already exhausted mounts. Heth's strong defensive position provided not only earthworks but also a panoramic view of the wood line and wide open fields in front of them on both sides of Falling Waters Road. Major Weber acknowledged his orders, saluted, mounted, and then barked commands to the officers and noncommissioned officers of Companies B and F who in turn repeated them to the troopers.

On the ridge and to the rear of the Donnelly house, Generals Heth and Pettigrew spotted a formation of horsemen advancing from the wood line nearly a mile away across a field. They moved deliberately toward and then onto Falling Waters Road in the direction of the rebel position. Raising their field glasses toward the approaching mounted troops, Heth and Pettigrew must have been baffled. A squadron of cavalry was drawn up in formation and advancing rapidly. Some historians have speculated Weber's men may have been wearing rubber rain ponchos which would have covered their blue uniform coats. Confederate horsemen also wore ponchos—captured from Federal cavalrymen and supply trains—though neither of the drawings of the July 14 action by artists Edwin Forbes or Alfred Waud depicts Weber's men wearing ponchos. Additionally, the rain had ceased by the time of the Weber's advance. At the head of the mounted formation, a Union cavalry guidon flew. Heth and Pettigrew concluded the horsemen were from Stuart's command and the guidon was a captured battle trophy from a skirmish with Union horsemen. Whether it was due to the mud, ponchos, or some other reason, the senior officers of Hill's rear guard were unable to clearly distinguish whether they were friend or foe as the cavalry advanced toward their position. To be cautious, Pettigrew ordered his men to assemble with their arms, which had been stacked, load, and prepare to fire. But the senior officer, Heth, was confident the horsemen were Stuart's so he countermanded Pettigrew's order.

No sooner had Pettigrew's order been reversed than Weber's two companies of Michigan cavalry wheeled from column into line and drew their glistening sabers. The situation suddenly became clear to Heth, Pettigrew, and the other officers and men atop the ridge. They did not know, contrary to orders, Stuart's cavalry under Fitzhugh Lee crossed into Virginia at Williamsport long before Hill's troops were across the Potomac River pontoon bridge at Falling Waters.

The two mounted companies of Michigan Wolverines led by Major Weber, sabers unsheathed, crossed from Falling Waters Road toward their right and rode across a section of a field bordering the road. The Wolverines' mounts struggled in the mud as they moved across the field and up the rise toward the rebels' defenses. As the officers and troopers reached the crest, they were met with a sheet of flame and deadly lead from Heth's troops, whose muskets were still serviceable in spite of the rain and mud. Once at the top of the rise, Weber and his officers and men could see for the first time the scale of Heth's rear guard force which had formed lines of battle in front of them, extending beyond sight to both the right and the left with additional troops in reserve only slightly to the rear as the ridge sloped back down toward a ravine beyond the Donnelly barn.

Those Michigan troopers and horses who survived the initial volley from Heth's line continued forward. They rode between or over the earthen emplacements which lined the crest of the rise but were vacant of artillery. As the remaining Wolverines cleared the emplacements, they faced hand-to-hand combat with the rebels. Heth's battle hardened veterans used their musket as clubs, swung fence rails, hurled stones, and even wielded axes against both the Michigan horsemen and their mounts. While some of the Confederates' rifles, muskets, and pistols were too muddy or wet to fire, those that were serviceable continued to do their lethal work against the survivors of Weber's two companies.

After piercing the very center of the rebel line, the Michigan horsemen guided their frothing mounts toward the right, along and to the rear of Heth's left. They continued to draw fire as they rode within Heth's lines. Soon, those Wolverines who were not dead, wounded, or captured retreated back down the rise, across the field, and toward Falling Waters Road to their original position near the tree line. Some of the Wolverine horsemen who returned were mounted and others were without their mounts. Riderless horses returned, too. The bold assault against Heth's position was suicidal for Weber's command. Weber, who had led the charge, was dead and so was his second in command, Lieut. Charles E. Bolza. Officers and men from the two companies paid the ultimate price for Kilpatrick's reckless order.

Officers and troopers in the two Michigan cavalry companies were not the only casualties during the clash. Pettigrew initially directed the defense from astride his horse outside the fenced garden to the rear of the Donnelly house. Between the garden fence and the Donnelly barn, approximately 50 yards behind and slightly to the left of the garden, he was thrown from his horse during the attack. Accounts of what happened next vary but several key elements are consistent.

Pettigrew had been wounded in the left hand on July 3 at Gettysburg. His right arm remained weak from a wound received earlier in the war. After being thrown from his horse, Pettigrew rose to his feet. The Confederate general saw a dismounted Michigan trooper near the barn firing at the defenders. Pettigrew drew the small pistol he carried and ordered his men shoot the Federal cavalryman. The noise combined with the smoke and confusion of battle must have made it impossible for the men to hear Pettigrew's command, so he stepped toward the Yankee cavalryman himself. Seeing a Confederate officer, pistol in hand, advancing in his direction, the Union trooper raised his weapon, aimed, and fired.

Pettigrew was struck in what some accounts describe as the abdomen and others the groin. Regardless, he received a grievous wound delivered at close range from a weapon with a large projectile. One of Pettigrew's men killed the Yankee on the spot. According to one account, the rebel soldier crushed the Yankee trooper with a large rock. At the time, Union horsemen were galloping up the length of and behind the Confederate line (to the left of where Pettigrew was struck). Heth's command was buoyed by their success in repelling the horsemen. It may have felt to them at the time like a bit of revenge for the terrible price they paid at Gettysburg only eleven days earlier. Exhilaration quickly turned to shock and anger as they learned Pettigrew lay severely wounded. As Heth's officers and men recovered from the attack, they began to prepare for the inevitable next one. The soldiers, no doubt, began to spread word along the battle line the brilliant Brigadier General Pettigrew had been wounded.

Additional elements of Kilpatrick's 3^d Division began to arrive from Williamsport. They formed near the tree line as the survivors of Weber's charge straggled back. Undeterred by the devastating losses to Weber's two companies, including Weber himself, Kilpatrick ordered another attack by his division toward Heth's position. Part of Kilpatrick's division was now ordered to advance on foot as skirmishers, as Custer had originally intended. Advancing on Heth's line, they were repelled. This attack was then followed by another with a larger mounted force. Led personally by Custer, they followed the same approach taken by Weber and his two companies. One can imagine Custer leading his horsemen from the front, shouting something inspirational to his Wolverines as they galloped toward Heth's position.

Troopers from John Buford's division arrived from the east in the vicinity of the fighting only after additional elements of Kilpatrick's division were engaged. Buford, having hoped to trap the rebels between the Kilpatrick's force and the river, must have felt a sense of frustration when he heard the familiar sounds of men and horses in deadly combat. Buford's troopers briefly halted their horses as they awaited their orders through Buford's chain of command. Still hoping to cut off and capture Heth's rear guard, Buford's division advanced from the east hitting Heth's flank and moving toward the ground that lay between the rebels and the river.

Although the combined Federal cavalry force outnumbered Heth's rear guard by approximately two to one, Heth's strong defensive position and the lack of coordination with Kilpatrick caused Buford's plan to snare the rebel rear guard to fail. Without Stuart's cavalry screen, with no operational artillery available, and with only half the men who had marched to Gettysburg in June still able to fight, Heth continued to obey his orders from Hill and held his position. The Battle of Falling Waters, Maryland, had evolved into more than an ill-advised charge by two companies of Michigan cavalry. And the fighting was not yet over.

Official Reports and First-Hand Accounts

Army of Northern Virginia

Lieut. Gen. Ambrose P. Hill recorded:

"Being the rear guard of the army, such dispositions as were necessary were made to repel any advance of the enemy. Anderson's division
crossed without molestation, and Pender's was in the act of crossing
when the enemy made their appearance. A small body of cavalry charged
Pettigrew's and Archer's brigades, and were annihilated."

In his report, Maj. Gen. Henry Heth noted:

"… About 11 o'clock, I received orders from General Hill to move
Pender's division across the river, following General Anderson's division,
and, after leaving one brigade of my division in line, to follow up the
movement of the corps as speedily as possible.

"About fifteen or twenty minutes after receiving these orders, and
while they were in progress of execution, a small body of cavalry, num-
bering not more than 40 or 45 men, made their appearance in our front,
where the road debouched from the woods previously described. I will
here remark, that when on the road, and some 2 or 3 miles from the position I now occupied, a large body of our cavalry passed by my command,
going to our rear. When the cavalry alluded to made its appearance, it
was at once observed by myself, General Pettigrew, and several members
of my staff, as well as many others. On emerging from the woods, the
party faced about, apparently acting on the defensive. Suddenly facing
my position, they galloped up the road, and halted some 175 yards from
my line of battle. From their maneuvering and the smallness of numbers,
I concluded it was a party of our own cavalry pursued by the enemy. In
this opinion I was sustained by all present. It was not until I examined
them critically with my glasses at a distance of not more than 175 yards
that I discovered they were Federal troops. The men had been restrained
from firing up to this time by General Pettigrew and myself. The command was now given to fire. At the same time, the Federal officer in
command gave the command to charge. The squad passed through the
intervals separating the epaulements, and fired several shots. In less than

three minutes all were killed or captured save two or three, who are said to have escaped. General Pettigrew received a wound in one of his hands at Gettysburg, in consequence of which he was unable to manage his horse, which reared and fell with him. It is probable when in the act of rising from the ground that he was struck by a pistol-ball in the left side, which, unfortunately for himself and his country, proved mortal. A soldier of the Seventh Tennessee Regiment was at the same time mortally wounded. This was the entire loss of my command from this charge; 33 of the enemy's dead were counted; 6 prisoners fell into our hands; also a stand of colors."

Lieut. Col. S. G. Shepherd, in command of Archer's Third Brigade, reported: "We moved on to within 2 miles of the river, and formed a line of battle upon the crest of a hill, to protect our rear until the artillery and the column in advance of us could cross the river. While here, a small squadron of the enemy's cavalry, consisting of 75 or 100 men, made their appearance in our front. They were mistaken at first for our own cavalry until they had advanced close upon us. Their first charge was upon the First Tennessee Regiment, which was upon the right of the brigade. Our men, unfortunately, did not have their guns all loaded, and were forced to fight with clubbed guns. The enemy, finding they were making rather slow headway at this point, moved down the line upon the Thirteenth Alabama, Seventh and Fourteenth Tennessee Regiments, who by this time had succeeded in getting many of their guns loaded, and were but a short time in killing and wounding a majority of them. The rest made a desperate effort to escape back to the woods, but most of those were shot from their horses as they fled, so that not over a dozen or twenty made their escape. We lost in this encounter 1 man killed and 7 wounded.

"It was our sad misfortune, too, in this affair, to lose General Pettigrew, who was in command of the brigade. No encomium that I might add could do justice to his memory. Both officers and men of the entire brigade feel that by his death the Confederacy has lost a model soldier and one of her most noble and gifted sons."

Lieut. Col. John J. Garnett (Heth's Division, Artillery) noted:
"On reaching the Virginia shore, I was ordered to place six of my pieces (two Napoleons and four rifled) in position on the hills to the left of the turnpike, and commanding the pontoon bridge, which I accordingly did."

Brig. Gen. James H. Lane, in command of Pender's Division, wrote in his report:
"Just as we were ordered to resume our march, the troops of Heth's division that occupied the breastworks in our rear as a rear guard were attacked by the enemy's cavalry."

Col. William L. J. Lowrance, in command of Scales' Fourth Brigade, recorded:
"... but just as we were moving out to cross the river, were attacked by a squad of cavalry, which caused some detention."

Lee's cavalry commander, Maj. Gen. J. E. B. Stuart, noted in his report:
"General Hill's troops being notified that these squadrons would follow in his rear, were deceived by some of the enemy's cavalry, who approached very near, in consequence of their belief that they were our cavalry. Although this unfortunate mistake deprived us of the lamented General Pettigrew, whom they mortally wounded, they paid the penalty of their temerity by losing most of their number in killed or wounded, if the accounts of those who witnessed it are to be credited. The cavalry crossed at the fords without serious molestation, bringing up the rear on that route by 8 a.m. on the 14th."

Army of the Potomac

Maj. Gen. George G. Meade noted in his report:
"The cavalry in pursuit overtook the rear guard at Falling Waters, capturing two guns and numerous prisoners."

Capt. Lemuel B. Norton, Chief Signal Officer, wrote:
"On July 14, the enemy were discovered to have crossed the river during the night before. At the close of this day all signal stations and lines were discontinued."

Brig. Gen. Henry J. Hunt (Chief of Artillery) reported:

"I received no report of captures from the enemy in an official form, although I heard that the cavalry had picked up several on the road, and that two were taken at Falling Waters."

Maj. Gen. Alfred Pleasonton (Cavalry Corps) submitted:

"On July 14, General Gregg, with McIntosh's and Gregg's brigades, of his division, crossed the Potomac at Harper's Ferry, and quickly drove a force of the enemy's cavalry back upon Charlestown. The entire rebel army having affected a crossing of the Potomac on that day, Gregg was re-enforced by Huey's brigade, and directed to gain the flank and rear of the rebels, and harass them as much as possible. He marched to Shepherdstown, found the roads to Martinsburg and Winchester strongly picketed, and Huey's brigade not having joined him, he waited until the 16th, when the enemy attacked him in force. A spirited contest was maintained until some time after dark, when the enemy withdrew. A large quantity of bacon and flour was captured by our troops at Shepherdstown. General Gregg speaks of the high soldierly qualities exhibited by his officers and men on that occasion.

"On July 14, both Buford's and Kilpatrick's divisions pursued the rebels to Falling Waters, capturing many prisoners; a good deal of abandoned property also fell into our hands. The enemy's rear guard made an obstinate resistance near Falling Waters, but was dispersed by General Kilpatrick, who took from them, among other trophies, three infantry battle-flags."

Brig. Gen. John Buford recorded:

"The division succeeded in getting the road, and attacked the enemy in flank and rear, doing him great damage, and scattering him in confusion through the woods and ravines. Our spoils on this occasion were one 10-pounder Parrott gun, one caisson, over 500 prisoners, and about 300 muskets."

Brig. Gen. Judson Kilpatrick stated in his official report:

"Within less than 1,000 yards of this large force, a second piece of artillery with its support (consisting of infantry) was captured while attempting to get into position. The gun was taken to the rear. A portion of the Sixth Michigan Cavalry, seeing only that portion of the enemy behind the earthworks, charged. This charge, led by Major Weber, was the most gallant ever made. At a trot he passed up the hill, received the fire from the whole line, and the next moment rode through and over the earthworks; passed to the right, sobering rebels along the entire line, and returned with a loss of 30 killed, wounded, and missing, including the gallant Major [P. A.] Weber killed. I directed General Custer to send forward one regiment as skirmishers. They were repulsed before support could be sent them, and driven back, closely followed by the rebels, until checked by the First Michigan and a squadron of the Eighth New York. The Second Brigade, having come up, was quickly thrown into position ..."

Brig. Gen. George A. Custer's report detailed by each of his units:
First Michigan Cavalry
    "On the 14th, this regiment was engaged in the action at Falling Waters."

Fifth Michigan Cavalry
    "(at Williamsport) ... and driving the enemy's rear guard across the river, capturing a number of prisoners."

Sixth Michigan Cavalry
    "July 14.—Was in the engagement at Falling Waters. Two companies—B and F, commanded by Major Weber—charged the enemy, who were in position behind earthworks on the crest of a hill. Major Weber and Lieutenant Bolza, with many valuable men, were killed."

Seventh Michigan Cavalry
    "July 14.—Was engaged on the right at Falling Waters ..."

Battery M, 2[d] U. S. Artillery
    "... shelling the enemy at the latter place, he being on the opposite side of the river. At Falling Waters the battery was employed throughout the day."

Chapter 6

July 14
Advance and Withdrawal at Falling Waters

Kilpatrick's growing force of horsemen, his mounted artillery, and the arrival of Buford's troopers created a dilemma for Heth and his rear guard. What began as an ill-advised charge by two companies of Michigan cavalry soon escalated into a full scale engagement for two of the Army of the Potomac's cavalry divisions. Heth knew more enemy combatants would soon arrive and join in the fighting. He was faced with the decision of how best to obey his orders and still have his division, so mauled eleven days earlier at Gettysburg, survive to cross the Potomac River.

According to one of the more recent detailed analyses of forces at Gettysburg, the approximate strength of Heth's Division before and after Gettysburg was as follows (John W. Busey and David G. Marin, *Regimental Strengths and Losses at Gettysburg*, p. 221):

Staff: 8
Pettigrew: 2,580 – 1,619 losses = 961
Davis: 2,305 – 1,225 losses = 1,080
Brockenbrough: 972 – 214 losses = 758
Archer: 1,197 – 684 losses = 513
(Garnett: 396 but was already across the Potomac River by the time of the attack)
Total Heth without Garnett: 7,062 – 3,742 losses = 3,320

The majority of Heth's infantry were armed with single shot, muzzle loading, rifled muskets which were the standard infantry weapon during the 1861–1865 war. These included imported English manufactured Enfield rifle muskets, weapons of Confederate manufacture, and captured Federal rifled muskets, some of which were manufactured at Springfield Arsenal in Massachusetts. It is not known how much ammunition the troops in the rear guard carried but we do know when they were attacked some of their weapons did not fire forcing them to "club" their muskets (swing them by the barrel like a baseball bat) with the butt toward their attackers. Even in the best of conditions, Heth's men would have been able to fire no more than three to four shots per minute by grabbing a cartridge from their cartridge box or pocket, tearing it open, putting the charge of gunpowder and lead bullet in the barrel, ramming it down the barrel, returning the rammer, pulling a percussion cap from their cap pouch or pocket, placing the fresh cap on the ignition nipple, cocking the hammer back, aiming, and firing. The effect of heavy rains and mud on the Confederate arms at this time may also have been a factor. All of the military muskets had fittings for either socket or sword bayonets, but we do not know how many of Heth's men had their bayonets with them in the scabbards worn at their left sides or fixed on the barrels of their muskets at this point of the Gettysburg Campaign. They had stacked their arms, which usually means their bayonets were "fixed."

The strength of the Federal cavalry under Buford and Kilpatrick before and after Gettysburg was (Busey and Marin, *Regimental Strengths,* p. 103):

Buford: 4,073 – 176 losses = 3,897
Kilpatrick: 3,892 – 355 losses = 3,537
Total combined Federal cavalry forces: 7,434

The figure for the combined Union cavalry force at Falling Waters was probably less than 7,434 due to the fact some of Kilpatrick's command may have remained in Williamsport at the river crossing since earlier in the morning. Also, we do not know how many of Kilpatrick's and Buford's troopers remained as camp guards, on picket duty, served as couriers, and in other capacities common to the cavalry while on campaign.

The armaments of the Union cavalry varied. Kilpatrick's command, including Custer's Wolverines, were armed with Sharps and Burnside carbines, Spencer rifles (specifically carried by the 5th and 6th Michigan), Colt .44 pistols,

Remington .44 pistols, Colt .36 pistols, and Whitney .36 pistols plus their long, curved regulation cavalry sabers. Buford's horsemen were armed with Sharps, Burnside, Smith, and Gallager carbines plus side arms including Colt .36, Colt .44, and Remington .36 revolvers. All of the Federal cavalry's carbines were breech-loading. Due to this armament, Kilpatrick's and Buford's troopers benefited from a higher rate of fire than the Confederate's muzzle loading rifled muskets (Busey and Marin, *Regimental Strengths,* pp. 157–8)

Much of what has been written about the Gettysburg Campaign dismisses the Battle of Falling Waters, Maryland, as a minor engagement between Heth's unprepared rear guard and two companies of Kilpatrick's cavalry. Contrary to that conclusion, Heth's force which had been decimated in combat at and after Gettysburg consisted of approximately 3,320 men. They did not have access to their artillery because, according to most accounts, it was already safely across the Potomac. Heth's troops faced a force double their size with approximately 7,434 horsemen plus supporting artillery. Heth's command was armed with single-shot rifled muskets, at least some of which were not functional by the morning of July 14. Buford and Kilpatrick's troopers' armament included breech loading carbines and rifles, revolvers, and sabers. They were supported by the range and killing force of field pieces. Even if Heth's men had been well-armed, well-fed, and rested, they could not repulse a force double their size with better weapons and supported by artillery for long, regardless of their excellent defensive position.

Additional blue-clad horsemen arrived on the battlefield. They attacked along Heth's defensive line and his flanks. Frontal attacks by skirmishers and mounted horsemen followed the repulse of Weber's Wolverines. Movements to attack Heth's flanks had the objective of cutting off his troops' ability to reach the pontoon bridge crossing. Heth grew increasingly concerned about the ability of his men to hold their rear guard position. Lane, whose command had not yet crossed the pontoon bridge, received orders by way of a messenger, to return back up Falling Waters Road to support the rear guard's position. Additionally, Heth requested that Hill recall his artillery which was already across the Potomac in Virginia. Hill had no desire to lose a single gun fighting a rear guard engagement in a campaign that was, from his perspective, already over. He denied Heth's request.

On the rear guard's right and across the road from the rise, was Brockenbrough's position. His command included the 22^d, 40th, 47th, and 55th Virginia Infantry. For reasons unknown, Brockenbrough ordered his men to attack across the open field to their front, the direction from which Kilpatrick's horsemen had launched their attacks. The Virginians advanced out from their defensive positions with their colors in the lead. Brockenbrough's movement was unsupported along the line. Incredibly, this occurred only eleven days after the disastrous charge at Gettysburg, which came to be known as Pickett's charge. Some of Brockenbrough's veterans must have recognized it was sheer folly to advance across an open field toward ever growing numbers of Federal cavalry on horse and foot supported by artillery. Outnumbered by the Yankees, many of Brockenbrough's officers, including Col. William Steptoe Christian of the 55th Virginia, and men were captured along with their colors and arms. Brockenbrough, rather than leading his troops from the front, withdrew in the direction of the Potomac River with some of his staff as his own troops attacked in accordance to his orders. The event would haunt him and leave his command shaken in the days ahead.

Most of Hill's corps, including the artillery's guns and ammunition, had crossed the Potomac River via the pontoon bridge and were now in Virginia. Hill, having refused Heth's request for artillery support, now ordered him to withdraw his division from their position. It must have seemed odd to Hill that Stuart's cavalry had not alerted Heth of the advancing Federal cavalry. Regardless, Heth's command had done its job by protecting the corps' rear as it crossed the Potomac. Now it was time for them to cross. Continuing the fight would only lead to additional losses of much needed men and materiel and was not in line with the Army of Northern Virginia's objectives at this point in the campaign.

A common misconception about the Battle of Falling Waters is that Heth's withdrawal was a disorganized dash to the pontoon bridge. Contrary to that misconception, upon receiving orders from Heth, Lane's Division advanced back up Falling Waters Road toward the position of the rear guard. They formed a line of battle on either side of the road to the rear of Heth's position. The military textbook movement was completed with discipline and speed in spite of the mud and heat of the mid-July day. Once Lane's men arrived, Heth's force began to withdraw from their positions. They formed successive lines of battle to the rear of Lane's Division which at the time was only armed with fixed bayonets on their muskets. The lines of battle were funneled into more compact formations and ultimately columns as the withdrawing troops moved down Falling Waters Road toward the pontoon bridge crossing. Lane's men continued the leap-frog movement with Heth's Division until they reached the ramp over the C&O Canal and then the pontoon bridge across the Potomac just beyond the canal.

As Heth's troops withdrew toward the river crossing, Kilpatrick's and Buford's horsemen continued their attack along the front and also the flanks of the withdrawing Confederates. Some rebel stragglers and wounded were captured. Officers and men actively fighting while en route to the pontoon bridge were also captured. This was particularly true for those who sought escape by way of the steep cliffs to the left of Heth's position. These dropped down to and along the C&O Canal. The sheer drop-off along the canal and river was choked with thick growth including vines which impeded the withdrawing rebels' progress. Some officers, attempting to lead their men to the river, became casualties themselves. From Lane's command, 3^d Lieut. Nathaniel S. Smith of the 13th North Carolina Infantry and 2^d Lieutenant John H. Burkin of the 22^d North Carolina Infantry of Brig. Gen. Alfred M. Scales' Brigade (under the command of Col. W. L. J. Lowrance) were among those captured at Falling Waters. In spite of the disciplined withdrawal, it was during the rear guard's movement toward the pontoon bridge crossing that Federal troopers captured more Confederates in addition to those captured from Brockenbrough's brigade of Virginians.

As Heth began to affect the withdrawal of his command from their defensive positions, Pettigrew lay grievously wounded near where he fell, in the rear of the Donnelly house between the garden and the barn. Surrounded by members of his staff and attended to by one of the surgeons, discussion took place as to whether Pettigrew should be moved or left to the care of the rapidly advancing Federals and their surgeons. Having previously suffered the consequences of being wounded and then captured, Pettigrew made clear he would not remain behind. As his troops began their movement down Falling Waters Road toward the Potomac, several soldiers, under the guidance of Pettigrew's staff, transported the wounded commander on a bone jarring trip. He was first moved down to the road, on to the crossing and then over the pontoon bridge. For the gravely wounded Pettigrew, it must have been an excruciating journey.

Soldiers from Heth's and Lane's commands finally reached and crossed the pontoon bridge over the Potomac at Falling Waters. Supporting artillery and sharpshooters on the Virginia side provided covering fire to keep the ever-increasing number of Yankee horsemen at bay. Federal artillery fired projectiles from their

Maryland positions toward the rebels. The last men to cross the pontoon bridge served in the 26th North Carolina of Pettigrew's brigade. Their final act as they stepped onto the pontoon bridge was to cut it free from the Maryland shore. Federal troopers, who had been solely focused on capturing the maximum number of Heth's and Lane's men arrived and gathered near the river bank. There they continued to face both rifle and artillery fire from the Virginia side. The horsemen in blue undoubtedly were overcome by exhaustion and frustration, perhaps mixed with a degree of relief. To both Heth's and Lane's officers and men, the sight of the pontoon bridge swinging free in the current of the Potomac River was a vivid symbol for the end of the summer 1863 invasion of Pennsylvania which became known as the Gettysburg Campaign.

Official Reports and First-Hand Accounts

Army of Northern Virginia

Gen. Robert E. Lee wrote:
"Brigadier-General Pettigrew was mortally wounded in an attack made by a small body of cavalry, which was unfortunately mistaken for our own, and permitted to enter our lines. He was brought to Bunker Hill, where he expired a few days afterward. He was a brave and accomplished officer and gentleman, and his loss will be deeply felt by the country and the army."

Lieut. Gen. Ambrose P. Hill recorded:
"Only 2 of ours killed; but, unfortunately for the service, one of them was the gallant and accomplished Pettigrew.

"Subsequently the enemy pressed on vigorously, and I directed General Heth to retire his troops and cross the river. In doing this, some loss was sustained, principally in stragglers, and not exceeding 500, composed of men from the various brigades of the army. Two pieces of artillery were broken down on this night march, and abandoned. Colonel Walker brought off three guns captured on the field of Gettysburg. "

In his report, Maj. Gen. Henry Heth noted:

"Very soon after this, a large body of dismounted cavalry, supported by artillery, of which I had none, made a vigorous attack on Brockenbrough's brigade, which was deployed in line of battle to the right of the road. Brockenbrough repelled the attack, and drove the enemy back into the woods, following him up for some distance. The enemy was now heavily re-enforced, and Brockenbrough was compelled to fall back.

"His brigade, having been badly cut up on the 1st and 3d at Gettysburg, was much reduced in numbers. Seeing that the enemy evidently designed turning his right flank, and thus cutting him off from the river, Brockenbrough deployed his brigade as skirmishers, extending well to the right. About this time the enemy appeared on my left flank in force; also in my front. Seeing the attack was becoming serious, I ordered the several brigades of Pender's division (excepting Thomas', which had crossed the river) to return. At the same time, I sent a message to the lieutenant-general commanding, requesting that artillery might be sent me, as I had none.

"On returning, my aide informed me that General Hill directed me to withdraw my command as speedily as possible and cross the river. When this order was received, my line of skirmishers occupied a front of a mile and a half, the left resting on the canal, the right bending around well toward the Potomac. The orders were that the several brigades in line should withdraw simultaneously, protecting their front by a strong line of skirmishers, and converge toward the road leading to Falling Waters. In order to cover this movement, Lane's brigade was formed in line of battle about 500 yards in rear of the advanced line, protected by a heavy line of skirmishers.

"The first brigade that passed through Lane's line of battle was re-formed in line of battle a quarter of a mile or more in rear of Lane's position, and so on till the command reached the south bank of the Potomac. With the extended line of skirmishers in my front, and being compelled to fall back upon a single road, it is not surprising that, in attempting to reach the road over ravines impassable at many points, and through a thick undergrowth and wood, and over a country with which both officers and men were unacquainted, many of them were lost, and thus fell into the hands of the enemy, who pushed vigorously forward on seeing that I was retiring. The enemy made two cavalry charges, and on each occasion I witnessed the unhorsing of the entire party.

"I desire here to brand upon its perpetrator a falsehood and correct an error. The commander of the Federal forces (General Meade) reported to his Government, on the statement of General Kilpatrick, that he (General Kilpatrick) had captured a brigade of infantry in the fight at Falling Waters. To this General Lee replied, in a note to General Cooper, that no organized command had been captured. General Meade recently wrote a note to his Government, reaffirming his first statement, upon the authority of General Kilpatrick. General Kilpatrick, in order to glorify himself, has told a deliberate falsehood. He knows full well that no organized body of men was captured; not even a company was captured, nor the majority of a single company. He asserts, however, that he captured an entire brigade.

"The error I wish to correct is attributing all the men captured by the enemy on the 14th as belonging to my command. I think I state correctly when I say that 3 out of 4 of the men captured by the enemy were captured between our works near Hagerstown and the point where I engaged the enemy, and were the representatives of every corps, division, and brigade which passed over this road. My staff officers alone succeeded in driving from barns and houses immediately on the roadside several hundred stragglers who probably never reached their commands, and these were but a small proportion of the men who straggled."

Lieut. Col. S. G. Shepherd, in command of Archer's Third Brigade, reported:
"We received orders to retire toward the river, and we moved out, with General Pettigrew's brigade upon our left. Our route to the river was part of the way through a dense and tangled copse of undergrowth, with deep ravines running up from the river. We kept our line pretty well organized in passing through these obstructions, and passed beyond the river."

Lieut. Col. John J. Garnett (Heth's Division, Artillery) noted:
"... and very soon thereafter, General Pendleton being present, they opened upon the enemy's skirmishers, and checked their advance upon the bridge. These pieces kept up an irregular fire until evening, when

I ordered them to cease firing, the enemy evincing no intention of attempting to cross, and their formations not being sufficiently large to warrant the further expenditure of ammunition."

Brig. Gen. James H. Lane, in command of Pender's Division, wrote in his report:

"I at once ordered my command to fix bayonets, as our guns were generally unloaded, and moved down the road after General Thomas, but was soon halted by General Heth's order, and subsequently made to take a position in line of battle, to allow those brigades that were engaged to withdraw. I threw out a very strong line of skirmishers along our whole front, under Lieutenant [James M.] Crowell, of the Twenty-eighth, with instructions not to fire until the enemy got close upon him, and to fall back gradually when he saw the main line retiring toward the river. The Eighteenth Regiment, under Colonel Barry, was deployed to the right as skirmishers, and Colonel Avery had supervision of the right wing, so as to enable me to be apprised of the movements of the enemy more readily. As soon as the other brigades withdrew, a large force moved to our right, and as our left was also threatened, I lost no time in falling back, which was done in excellent order.

"Our thanks are due to Lieutenant Crowell and the officers and men under him for the stubbornness with which they contested every inch of ground against the enemy's mounted and dismounted cavalry, thereby enabling us to effect a crossing without the brigade being engaged. Lieutenant Crowell's command was the last organized body to cross the bridge."

Col. William L. J. Lowrance, in command of Scales' Fourth Brigade, recorded:

"Then, all being quiet, I moved off, as directed, toward the river, but ere I had gone more than 300 yards, I was ordered by General Heth to take the brigade back to the support of those who were acting as rear guard; and, having done so, I took a position on the right of the center, which point appeared to be threatened, but was immediately ordered by General Heth to form the brigade on the extreme left; and having formed the brigade, as directed, by moving there in quick time (being informed that that point was threatened), I found the men were quite exhausted from pressure of heat, want of sleep, want of food, and the fatigue of marching; and at this very moment I found the troops on our right giving way, whereupon I sent Lieutenant [J. D.] Young, acting aide-de-camp, to rally them, which he did after some time. Then I was ordered to join on their right, and, while making a move to this effect, ere we had come to the top of the hill on which they were, I rode forward, and saw the whole line in full retreat some 200 or 300 yards to my rear; the enemy were pursuing, and directly between me and the bridge.

"The move, I understand since, was made by order, but I received no such orders, in consequence of which I was cut off. But I filed directly to the rear, and struck the river some three-quarters of a mile above the bridge, and then marched down the river; but the enemy had penetrated the woods, and struck the river between us and the bridge, and so cut off many of our men who were unwilling to try to pass, and captured many more who failed from mere exhaustion; so in this unfortunate circumstance we lost nearly 200 men."

Lee's chief of artillery, Brig. Gen. W. N. Pendleton, reported:
"A few only of his guns, however, approached, and threw a shell or two, though they took care to keep out of view. A small body of skirmishers, besides, ventured rather nearer, but they were speedily dispersed by some well-directed shots, and cannon were there needed no longer."

Of the events on July 14, topographer Jedidiah Hotchkiss recorded:
"The infantry commenced crossing the river at 1 A.M. to-day—Longstreet first crossing the pontoon and A. P. Hill behind him leaving a rear guard. Ewell's Corps waded the river at Williamsport, the water reaching up to the arm-pits of the men. It was said that we lost 8,000 pairs of shoes in crossing. Everything came safely over and the cavalry crossing soon this morning. The enemy's cavalry came on and surprised some of Hill's men but suffered in consequence when they rallied. The enemy fired his artillery at our cavalry after they had cross at Williamsport. General Ewell came up to our camp at 4 A.M. and

we moved to a dry place in the woods, the camp named 'Stephens' by General Jackson June 20th 1861. The day was quite pleasant and we all dried ourselves. Johnson's division encamped near us. Rodes and Early back towards Falling Waters." (Hotchkiss, *Make Me a Map*, p. 161)

Army of the Potomac

Maj. Gen. George G. Meade noted in his report:
"The cavalry in pursuit overtook the rear guard at Falling Waters, capturing two guns and numerous prisoners."

Capt. Lemuel B. Norton, Chief Signal Officer, wrote:
"At the close of this day all signal stations and lines were discontinued."

Brig. Gen. Henry J. Hunt (Chief of Artillery) reported:
"I received no report of captures from the enemy in an official form, although I heard that the cavalry had picked up several on the road, and that two were taken at Falling Waters."

Maj. Gen. Alfred Pleasonton (Cavalry Corps) submitted:
"On July 14, both Buford's and Kilpatrick's divisions pursued the rebels to Falling Waters, capturing many prisoners; a good deal of abandoned property also fell into our hands. The enemy's rear guard made an obstinate resistance near Falling Waters, but was dispersed by General Kilpatrick, who took from them, among other trophies, three infantry battle-flags."

Brig. Gen. John Buford recorded:
"General Merritt came up in time to take the advance before the enemy had entirely crossed, and made many captures. The enemy's bridge was protected by over a dozen guns in position and sharpshooters on the Virginia side. As our troops neared the bridge, the enemy cut the Maryland side loose, and the bridge swung to the Virginia side."

Brig. Gen. Judson Kilpatrick stated in his official report:

"... and, after a fight of two hours and a half, we routed the enemy at all points, and drove him toward the river. When within a short distance of the brigade, General Buford's command came up and took the advance. We lost 29 killed, 36 wounded, and 40 missing. We found upon the field 125 dead rebels, and brought away upward of 50 wounded. A large number of the enemy's wounded was left upon the field, in charge of their own surgeons. We captured 2 guns, 3 battle-flags, and upward of 1,500 prisoners. To General Custer and his brigade, Lieutenant Pennington and his battery, and one squadron of the Eight New York Cavalry, of General Buford's command, all praise is due."

Brig. Gen. George A. Custer's report detailed by each of his units:
First Michigan Cavalry

"... and had the honor of capturing 2 battle-flags and so much of the Forty-seventh Regiment Virginia Infantry as was upon the field, being 5 officers and 56 men."

Sixth Michigan Cavalry

"Two companies—B and F, commanded by Major Weber—charged the enemy, who were in position behind earthworks on the crest of a hill. Major Weber and Lieutenant Bolza, with many valuable men, were killed."

Seventh Michigan Cavalry

"... capturing from the enemy a 10-pounder Parrott gun, 400 prisoners, the battle-flag of the Fifty-fifth Virginia Infantry, and the colonel of the above named regiment, with several other officers."

Battery M, 2^d U. S. Artillery

"... shelling the enemy at the latter place, he being on the opposite side of the river. At Falling Waters the battery was employed throughout the day."

James Henry Avery of the 5th Michigan Cavalry wrote:

"We next took up our march for Falling Waters, where we again arrived in time to get a parting salute and where we found there had been a terrible battle. The Sixth had charged into the rebel works, and captured a whole brigade; and as only two companies, F and B led the advance and were not supported properly, the rebs seized their guns and shot down most of them. Captain Weber was among the killed. This was the last fight of the great summer campaign of 1863, called the Gettysburg Campaign." (Avery, *Under Custer's Command,* p. 43)

Chapter 7

July 15–20
After Lee's Crossing of the Potomac

The period from July 15 through July 20 was one of movement for both the Army of Northern Virginia and the Army of the Potomac. Lee's forces, having crossed into Virginia, continued their march southward where they could rest and resupply after the brutal Gettysburg Campaign. Their journey was punctuated with tragedy. For Meade's army, the deliberate pace that accentuated the period following July 4 continued after July 14 with the exception, again, of the cavalry. During this time, Washington's glowing support for Meade turned into harsh criticism. In turn, Lee took the unusual step of publicly disputing reports attributed to his enemy in the media. It was during this same period that violent and destructive draft riots in many northern cities diverted the attention of the public from the events of July 14 in Maryland.

After crossing the Potomac River on July 14, Heth's command continued their march southward. They encamped five miles beyond the Falling Waters crossing point. By the evening of July 15 they had reached the town of Bunker Hill in what is now West Virginia. The Army of Northern Virginia remained there through July 21. During this period, the losses from both the battles in Pennsylvania and those in Maryland, including the one just prior to the crossing of the Potomac, became most evident. Heth's losses from not only the killed but also stragglers, those captured, and the wounded greatly thinned the ranks of his command. This was especially true among the North Carolina and Virginia regiments.

During this period, Heth's wounded Brigadier General Pettigrew spent his last days. Having been shot in the abdomen and ignoring the surgeon's pleas to stay behind in Maryland, he survived the ordeal of being transported down Falling Waters Road and across the pontoon bridge over the Potomac back to Virginia. On July 15, he was moved by wagon to Bunker Hill. Once at Bunker Hill, the gravely wounded Pettigrew was quartered in the Boyd home and was visited by surgeons who were unable to do anything to heal his severe gunshot wound. An Episcopal minister joined members of his staff at the bedside. He died from the wound received at Falling Waters, Maryland, on July 17. If not one of the great generals, the South lost one of its great intellects on that day. In spite of the heavy casualties during the Gettysburg Campaign, including many general officers, it is notable Lee and other Confederate leaders mourned the loss of Pettigrew. They referenced his passing in both official reports and personal correspondence.

The Army of the Potomac began pursuing Lee's Army of Northern Virginia again via Berlin (now Brunswick), Maryland, on July 15. The crossing was well south of Williamsport, closer to Middletown (a base of operations for Meade) and nearby Frederick. At Berlin, Meade's army briefly established a new headquarters. After crossing the Potomac on pontoon bridges, the Army of the Potomac moved its headquarters to Lovettsville, Virginia, on July 18 and then on to Wheatland on July 19. By July 20, the Army of the Potomac had moved deeply into Virginia's Shenandoah Valley. The cavalry crossed the Potomac at Berlin in advance of the main body of Meade's army. After crossing the river, they trailed Lee's army, including Stuart's cavalry. Similar to the period after July 3, following the July 15 crossing by the Army of the Potomac's cavalry, the horsemen participated in a number of skirmishes which are outside of the scope of this work. Rather than chasing the rebels in Virginia, Kilpatrick was temporarily reassigned to assist in quelling the draft riots which had erupted in New York City beginning on July 13. Rather than a slap on the wrist for the reckless disregard for his men at Gettysburg and then Falling Waters, he was personally favored by and selected for the duty by President Lincoln himself.

Army of the Potomac commander George Meade was occupied July 14 through 20 with messages from Washington which were both constant and critical of his actions. On July 14, the victor of Gettysburg received a steady stream of telegraphed messages from the War Department communicating President Lincoln's call for swift action to destroy Lee's army before it crossed the Potomac

River. News received at the War Department and the White House that same day informing the administration Lee had escaped into Virginia left the President angry and depressed.

General-in-Chief Henry Halleck telegraphed to Meade:
"The enemy should be pursued and cut up, wherever he may have gone ... I cannot advise details, as I do not know where Lee's army is, or where your pontoon bridges are.

"I need hardly to say to you that the escape of Lee's army without another battle has created great dissatisfaction in the mind of the President, and it will require an active and energetic pursuit on your part to remove the impression that it has not been sufficiently active heretofore." (Anders, *Halleck's War*, p. 459)

Meade, in turn, responded to Halleck:
"Having performed my duty conscientiously and to the best of my ability, the censure of the President conveyed in your dispatch of 1 P.M. this day, is, in my judgment, so undeserved that I feel compelled most respectfully to ask to be immediately relieved from the command of the army." (Anders, *Halleck's War*, p. 459)

Lincoln's feelings about the escape of Lee's army into Virginia without a battle are found in the words of a letter to Meade which the president wrote but decided not to send. It read in part:
"... you stood and let the river run down, bridges be built, and the enemy move away at his leisure without attacking him.

"Again, my dear General, I do not believe you appreciate the magnitude of the disaster involved in Lee's escape. He was within your easy grasp, and to have closed upon him would, in connection with our other successes (the capture of Vicksburg), have ended the war. As it is the war will be prolonged indefinitely ... Your golden opportunity is gone, and I am immeasurably distressed by it." (Anders, *Halleck's War*, p. 460)

Beyond the words in the unsent letter, the impact of Lee's escape on the president was noted by John Hay, Lincoln's secretary, who noted in his diary on July 15:

> "R.T.L. (the President's son Robert Todd Lincoln) says the President is grieved silently but deeply about the escape of Lee. He said 'If I had gone up there I could have whipped them myself.' I know he had that idea."
> (Hay, *Inside Lincoln's White House,* p. 63)

Although Meade remained in command of the Army of the Potomac, he never regained the faith or support of President Lincoln he had achieved immediately after July 3. The general who had led the Union victory at Vicksburg, Maj. Gen. Ulysses Grant, would be ordered east to take overall command of the Northern forces in the field. Meade's actions following July 3 would serve to define and diminish his role for the remainder of the conflict.

The Army of Northern Virginia's commander, Lee, wrote to his wife, Mary, from Bunker Hill on July 15. It was the first known correspondence to her since July 12. In his letter, he touched on and summarized some of the events of the previous days but was careful not to mention any of the casualties:

> "The army has returned to Virginia dear Mary. Its return is rather sooner than I had originally contemplated, but having accomplished what I proposed on leaving the Rappahannock, viz., relieving the Valley of the presence of the enemy & drawing his army north of the Potomac, I determined to recross the latter river. The enemy after concentrating his forces in our front began to fortify himself in his position, bring up his local troops, militia, &c., & all those around Washington & Alexandria. This gave him enormous odds. It also circumscribed our limits for procuring subsistence for men & animals, which with the uncertain stage of the river rendered it too hazardous for us to continue on the north side. It has been raining ever since we first crossed the Potomac. Making the roads horrid & embarrassing our operations. The night we recrossed it we got all over safe. Save such vehicles as broke down on the road from the mud, rocks, &c. We are all well. I hope will yet be able to damage our adversaries when they meet us, & that all will go right with us …"
> (*The Wartime Papers of R. E. Lee,* Edited by Clifford Dowdey and Louis H. Manarin, p. 551)

On July 16, in his official capacity, Lee wrote to Confederate President Jefferson Davis from Bunker Hill:

"... The army is encamped around this place, where we shall rest today. The men are in good health and spirits, but want shoes and clothing badly. I have sent back to endeavor to procure a supply of both, and also horseshoes, for want of which nearly half our cavalry is unserviceable. As soon as these necessary articles are obtained we shall be prepared to resume operations.

"I shall not need the pontoon train now, as the boats used at Falling Waters have been brought away, excepting the new ones constructed by us, which were too heavy and too large for transportation. I have accordingly ordered the train of which you speak to come no farther.

"... I learn that the enemy has thrown a pontoon bridge over the Potomac at Harper's Ferry. Should he follow us in this direction, I shall lead him up the Valley and endeavor to attack him as far from his base as possible." (*Wartime Papers of Lee,* p. 552)

Federal reports of the Battle of Falling Waters were printed in newspapers and brought to the attention of Lee. One such report was printed on July 25, 1863, in the popular *Harper's Weekly:*

"THE ENEMY ACROSS THE POTOMAC.

"General Meade telegraphs, July 14, my cavalry now occupy Falling Waters, having overtaken and captured a brigade of infantry 1500 strong, two guns, two caissons, two battle flags, and a large number of small-arms. The enemy are all across the Potomac."

Lee reacted to the newspaper accounts of his army's final engagement during the movement from Pennsylvania to Virginia. He viewed them as inaccurate and even took the time to respond to them. In a letter to the adjutant and inspector general, Gen. Samuel Cooper, he wrote:

"I have seen in the Northern papers what purported to be an official dispatch of General Meade, stating that he had captured a brigade of infantry, two pieces of artillery, two caissons, and a large number of small arms, as this army retired to the south bank of the Potomac on the 13th and 14th instant.

"This dispatch has been copied into the Richmond papers, and as its official character may cause it to be believed, I desire to state that it is incorrect. The enemy did not capture any organized body of men on that occasion, but only stragglers and such as were left asleep on the road, exhausted by the fatigue and exposure of one of the most inclement nights I have ever known at this season of the year. It rained without cessation, rendering the road by which our troops marched to the bridge at Falling Waters very difficult to pass, and causing so much delay that the last of the troops did not cross the river at the bridge until 1 p.m. on the 14th. While the column was thus detained on the road, a number of men, worn down with fatigue, lay down in barns and by the roadside, and though officers were sent back to arouse them as the troops moved on, the darkness and rain prevented them from finding all, and many were in this way left behind.

"Two guns were left in the road. The horses that drew them became exhausted and the officers went forward to procure others. When they returned, the rear of the column had passed the guns so far that it was deemed unsafe to send back for them and they were thus lost. No arms, cannon, or prisoners were taken by the enemy in battle, but only such as were left behind under the circumstances I have described. The number of stragglers thus lost I am unable to state with accuracy, but it is greatly exaggerated in the dispatch referred to." (*Wartime Papers of Lee*, pp. 557–8)

Later relating to the captured Confederates and Lee's reaction to the previous newspaper accounts of the Battle of Falling Waters, *Harper's Weekly* on September 5, 1863, noted:

"Four hundred more rebels, captured at Falling Waters and incarcerated in a prison in Baltimore, left that city the other day for Point Lookout. This makes nine hundred prisoners, now at Point Lookout, captured at the battle of Falling Waters, which Lee says was never fought!" (*Harper's Weekly, A Journal of Civilization*, Vol. VII, No. 349, New York, Saturday, September 5, 1863, p. 563)

Lee's stature as a military leader has varied over the many years since the war but he has nearly always been characterized as the model of southern virtue from boyhood to West Point, throughout his U. S. Army and Confederate military careers, and after as the president of Washington College. It appears from the letter to the adjutant and inspector general that Lee worried about what the newspapers reported regarding his army and their performance in battle in the summer of 1863. In response to newspaper reports about the July 14, 1863, Battle of Falling Waters, Lee was evidently willing to stretch the truth (or perhaps even outright lie) to preserve his reputation which had already damaged due to a less than favorable outcome at Gettysburg.

Within the month, Lee would send a letter of resignation to Confederate President Davis noting the criticism he had received following the Gettysburg Campaign in addition to his declining health. Davis refused to accept Lee's offer to resign.

In addition to the potential damage to Lee's reputation, it must be considered the attack by Federal cavalry at Falling Waters might never have occurred if Lee's own nephew, Fitzhugh Lee, obeyed his orders and maintained the buffer between Meade's forces and Hill's rear guard. Because Fitzhugh Lee crossed the Potomac River prematurely, he left Heth's command with a false sense of security. For this lapse, Lee the commander must surely have been embarrassed, if not angry. Rather than reprimand his nephew, Lee recommended him for a promotion. Fitzhugh Lee was promoted from brigadier general to major general not long after the Battle of Falling Waters.

For Robert E. Lee the Battle of Falling Waters resulted in the loss of the brilliant Brigadier General Pettigrew, additional troops being captured, and demonstrated fellow Virginian Brockenbrough, who chose to abandon his men while they were engaged in combat, was unfit to continue as a senior commander in the Army of Northern Virginia.

For George Meade, Falling Waters could have provided a modest victory related to Lee's retreat from Gettysburg and back across the Potomac River. In fact, the battle at Falling Waters highlighted for President Lincoln his still new commander of the Army of the Potomac had the appearance of having done too little, too late. Historians have argued since that time Lincoln's view may not have been realistic due to the condition of Meade's army, his primary orders to protect Washington, and Lee's strong defensive position. Regardless, Meade and the Army of the Potomac failed to deliver a crushing blow in Maryland and thus allowed the Army of Northern Virginia to return to the South.

Official Reports and First-Hand Accounts

Army of Northern Virginia

Gen. Robert E. Lee wrote:

"Brigadier-General Pettigrew was mortally wounded in an attack made by a small body of cavalry, which was unfortunately mistaken for our own, and permitted to enter our lines. He was brought to Bunker Hill, where he expired a few days afterward. He was a brave and accomplished officer and gentleman, and his loss will be deeply felt by the country and the army.

"The following day the army marched to Bunker Hill, in the vicinity of which it encamped for several days. The day after its arrival, a large force of the enemy's cavalry, which had crossed the Potomac at Harper's Ferry, advanced toward Martinsburg. It was attacked by General Fitz. Lee, near Kearneysville, and defeated with heavy loss, leaving its dead and many of its wounded on the field.

"Owing to the swollen condition of the Shenandoah, the plan of operations which had been contemplated when we recrossed the Potomac could not be put into execution, and before the waters had subsided, the movements of the enemy induced me to cross the Blue Ridge and take position south of the Rappahannock, which was accordingly done.

"As soon as the reports of the commanding officers shall be received, a more detailed account of these operations will be given, and occasion will then be taken to speak more particularly of the conspicuous gallantry and good conduct of both officers and men.

"It is not yet in my power to give a correct statement of our casualties, which were severe, including many brave men, and an unusual proportion of distinguished and valuable officers. Among them I regret to mention the following general officers: Major-Generals Hood, Pender, and Trimble severely, and Major-General Heth slightly wounded ...

"General Pettigrew, though wounded at Gettysburg, continued in command until he was mortally wounded, near Falling Waters."

Lieut. Gen. Ambrose P. Hill recorded:
"On the 21st, the march was resumed toward Culpeper Court-House. On the 23d, Wright's brigade, under Colonel Walker, was left to guard Manassas Gap until relieved by General Ewell. This brigade was attacked while there by an overwhelming force of the enemy, but held its ground stubbornly until relieved by Ewell's corps, when it marched with him to Culpeper. General Ewell speaks in high terms of the admirable conduct of this brigade ..."

In his report, Maj. Gen. Henry Heth noted:
"In conclusion, I will add that the brigade commanders did their duty, and the losses sustained were not attributable to any errors or shortcomings of theirs, but resulted from causes beyond their control. The rear guard of a large army protecting its crossing over a wide river can seldom fail to lose heavily if vigorously pursued by the enemy, especially when in the act of crossing. Under the circumstances, attacked as we were by a large and momentarily increasing force, we have every reason to be thankful that our losses were so small."

Lieut. Col. S. G. Shepherd, in command of Archer's Third Brigade, reported:
"It was our sad misfortune, too, in this affair, to lose General Pettigrew, who was in command of the brigade. No encomium that I might add could do justice to his memory. Both officers and men of the entire brigade feel that by his death the Confederacy has lost a model soldier and one of her most noble and gifted sons."

Lieut. Col. John J. Garnett (Heth's Division, Artillery) noted:
"The subsequent movements of my battalion are identical with those of the corps to which it is attached until we reached near Front Royal, when, in obedience to orders received through you, I turned off at that point, and proceeded up the Valley pike, by New Market, to this place, where my command is now conveniently encamped, having arrived here at 3 p.m. on the 29th ultimo by easy marches.

"I regret to state that the losses which my battalion has incurred during the recent campaign are especially heavy in horses, those now remaining being for the present almost totally unserviceable. It is my opinion, however, that with a short respite I will soon be able to report them as serviceable. I would respectfully state that, at the time of leaving Fredericksburg, their condition was generally bad, in consequence of the hardships they had encountered during the past winter, together with what they had gone through during the spring campaign."

Brig. Gen. James H. Lane, in command of Pender's Division, wrote in his report:

"Our loss in bringing up the rear was 6 wounded and 38 missing. Our entire loss in the trans-Potomac campaign was 731."

Col. William L. J. Lowrance, in command of Scales' Fourth Brigade, recorded: "Having recrossed the Potomac, we moved, as did the division, without any engagement until we came to Culpeper Court-House, Va., where the Thirty-fourth was engaged in a skirmish with the enemy's cavalry on August 1. Our loss, 3 wounded and some missing.

"In all this campaign, the men endured with their usual forbearance, and bore all their trials and privations without a murmur. It is proper to mention the conduct of Captain [Hugh L.] Guerrant, assistant adjutant and inspector general, Adjutant [D. M.] McIntire, acting assistant adjutant-general, and Lieutenant Young, acting aide-de-camp, who on all occasions rendered their services indispensable."

Maj. Gen. J. E. B. Stuart wrote in his report:
"To Baker's (late Hampton's) brigade was assigned the duty of picketing the Potomac from Falling Waters to Hedgesville. The other brigades were moved back toward Leetown, Robertson's being sent to the fords of the Shenandoah, where he already had a picket, which, under Captain [L. A.] Johnson, of the North Carolina cavalry, had handsomely repulsed the enemy in their advance on Ashby's Gap, inflicting severe loss, with great disparity in numbers.

"Harper's Ferry was again in possession of the enemy, and Colonel Harman, Twelfth Virginia Cavalry, had in an engagement with the enemy gained a decided success, but was himself captured by his horse falling.

"Upon my arrival at the Bower that afternoon (15th), I learned that a large force of the enemy's cavalry was between Shepherdstown and Leetown, and determined at once to attack him in order to defeat any designs he might have in the direction of Martinsburg.

"I made disposition accordingly, concentrating cavalry in his front, and early on the 16th moved Fitz. Lee's brigade down the turnpike, toward Shepherdstown, supported by Chambliss, who, though quite ill, with that commendable spirit which has always distinguished him, remained at the head of his brigade. Jenkins' brigade was ordered to advance on the road from Martinsburg toward Shepherdstown, so as by this combination to expose one of the enemy's flanks, while Jones, now near Charlestown, was notified of the attack, in order that he might co-operate. No positive orders were sent him, as his precise locality was not known.

"These dispositions having been arranged, I was about to attack when I received a very urgent message from the commanding general to repair at once to his headquarters. I therefore committed to Brig. Gen. Fitz. Lee the consummation of my plans, and reported at once to the commanding general, whom I found at Bunker Hill. Returning in the afternoon, I proceeded to the scene of conflict on the turnpike, and found that General Fitz. Lee had, with his own and Chambliss' brigades, driven the enemy steadily to within a mile of Shepherdstown, Jenkins' brigade not having yet appeared on the left. However, it soon after arrived in Fitz. Lee's rear, and moved up to his support. The ground was not practicable for cavalry, and the main body was dismounted, and advanced in line of battle. The enemy retired to a strong position behind stone fences and barricades, near Colonel [A. R.] Boteler's residence, and it being nearly dark, obstinately maintained his ground at this last point until dark, to cover his withdrawal.

"Preparations were made to renew the attack vigorously next morning, but daybreak revealed that the enemy had retired toward Harper's Ferry.

"The enemy's loss in killed and wounded was heavy. We had several killed and wounded, and among the latter Col. James H. Drake, First Virginia Cavalry, was mortally wounded, dying that night (16th), depriving his regiment of a brave and zealous leader, and his country of one of her most patriotic defenders.

"The commanding general was very desirous of my moving a large portion of my command at once into Loudoun, but the recent rains had so swollen the Shenandoah that it was impossible to ford it, and cavalry scouting parties had to swim their horses over.

"In the interval of time from July 16 to the 22d, the enemy made a demonstration on Hedgesville, forcing back Baker's brigade. Desultory skirmishing was kept up on that front for several days with the enemy, while our infantry was engaged in tearing up the Baltimore and Ohio Railroad near Martinsburg. Parts of Jones' brigade were also engaged with the enemy in spirited conflicts not herein referred to, resulting very creditably to our arms, near Fairfield, Pa., and on the Cavetown road from Hagerstown, the Sixth and Seventh Virginia Cavalry being particularly distinguished. Accounts of these will be found in the reports of Brigadier-General Jones and Colonel Baker ...

"I desire to mention among the brigadier-generals one whose enlarged comprehensions of the functions of cavalry, whose diligent attention to the preservation of its efficiency, and intelligent appreciation and faithful performance of the duties confided to him, point to as one of the first cavalry leaders on the continent, and richly entitle him to promotion. I allude to Brig. Gen. Fitz. Lee."

Lee's Chief of Artillery, Brig. Gen. W. N. Pendleton, reported:
"After crossing, Carter's guns were placed in position on the hill just below the bridge, and some of Garnett's on that just above. Lane's 20-pounder Parrotts were also posted some distance farther down, and [W. B.] Hurt's Whitworths higher up, all to repel an expected advance of the enemy. A few only of his guns, however, approached, and threw a shell or two, though they took care to keep out of view. A small body of skirmishers, besides, ventured rather nearer, but they were speedily dispersed by some well-directed shots, and cannon were there needed no longer.

"Besides the two serviceable guns mentioned as lost from failure of teams near the Potomac, the enemy got three of our disabled pieces, of which two were left on the field as worthless, and one sent to the rear was captured by his cavalry, with a few wagons from the train. We wrested from him, on the battlefield at Gettysburg, three 10-pounder Parrotts, one 3-inch rifle, and three Napoleons, all ready for use against himself."

Topographer Jedediah Hotchkiss recorded in his diary:
"Wednesday, July 15th. Orders were (given) to march at 8 a.m., but the First and Third Corps did not get by, so we did not march until in the afternoon when Johnson's division went to Darkesville, but Rodes stopped at the Big Spring, three miles from Martinsburg, and Early behind him. Longstreet and Hill went on to Bunkers Hill. We encamped, quite late, at Big Spring. I spent part of the day at Colonel James Faulkner's. A fine warm day." (Hotchkiss, *Make Me a Map*, p. 161)

Lieut. Col. William R. Carter of the 3[d] Virginia Cavalry wrote:
"July 15: Moved this morning one mile to get grazing for our horses, going into camp for a while. We were fortunate enough here to get a few barrels of corn, though this country has been pretty generally devastated by both armies. At 2 P.M. marched via Leetown towards Rippon & encamped near the turnpike from Charlestown to Smithfield." (Carter, *Sabres*, p. 83)

Army of the Potomac

Maj. Gen. George G. Meade noted in his report:
"Previous to the retreat of the enemy, Gregg's division of cavalry was crossed at Harper's Ferry, and, coming up with the rear of the enemy at Charlestown and Shepherdstown, had a spirited contest, in which the enemy was driven to Martinsburg and Winchester and pressed and harassed in his retreat. The pursuit was resumed by a flank movement, the army crossing the Potomac at Berlin and moving down the Loudoun Valley. The cavalry were immediately pushed into the several passes of the Blue Ridge, and, having learned from scouts the withdrawal of the Confederate army from the lower valley of the Shenandoah, the army, the Third Corps, Major-General French, in advance, was moved into the Manassas Gap, in the hope of being able to intercept a portion of the enemy.

"The possession of the gap was disputed so successfully as to enable the rear guard to withdraw by way of Strasburg, the Confederate army retiring to the Rapidan. A position was taken with this army on the line of the Rappahannock, and the campaign terminated about the close of July."

Capt. Lemuel B. Norton, Chief Signal Officer, wrote:

"On July 15, the headquarters of the army moved to Berlin. A signal station was opened at that place, communicating with a lookout station on Maryland Heights. This line remained in operation until the 18th.

"On July 16, the signal telegraph line was run from general headquarters to the Eleventh Corps headquarters, 1½ miles distant. Two officers were sent to make a telescopic reconnaissance from Loudoun Heights. Their reports were transmitted to the general commanding by orderly.

"On July 17, communication was opened by flag signals between headquarters at Berlin and an outpost station at Point of Rocks. An officer was sent to occupy a point of observation on Short Mountain.

"On July 18, general headquarters moved to Lovettsville, Va. A line of flag signals was worked between the Third and Fifth Corps.

"On July 19, headquarters of the army were moved to Wheatland, and communication established from thence to the lookout station on Short Mountain, and also between that mountain and the Fifth Corps headquarters.

"On July 20, the general headquarters moved to Union, and in the evening signals by torch were worked between that place and a station of observation at Snicker's Gap, on the Blue Ridge. The whereabouts and movements of the enemy in the Shenandoah Valley were discovered and correctly reported to the commanding general by the officers on this station. A party was ordered to open station and make a reconnaissance at Ashby's Gap. They arrived at that point at 8 p.m., but for some undiscovered reason failed to open communication with general headquarters during the night."

Brig. Gen. Henry J. Hunt (Chief of Artillery) reported:

"I received no report of captures from the enemy in an official form, although I heard that the cavalry had picked up several on the road, and that two were taken at Falling Waters."

Maj. Gen. Alfred Pleasonton (Cavalry Corps) submitted:

"On July 15, Buford's and Kilpatrick's divisions moved to Berlin to obtain supplies. Here the campaign of Gettysburg properly ended. The pursuit of the rebel army through Loudoun Valley to the Rappahannock River was made by the cavalry in detachments, of whose movements the reports of the division and brigade commanders give full details.

"In reviewing the conduct of the cavalry corps in this campaign, it becomes a proud gratification to call the attention of the major-general commanding to the devoted spirit and resolution that animated the officers and men throughout all the difficulties, privations, trials, and dangers they had constantly to meet, and which they overcame so gloriously. Not a single mishap occurred to mar the recollection of their noble and brilliant deeds.

"A report of this kind can only mention the names of those in position and for distinguished service, but I cordially indorse all the recommendations of the subordinate commanders. Brigadier-Generals Buford, Gregg, and Kilpatrick have proved themselves distinguished as division commanders, and I tender to them my warmest thanks for the intelligence and harmony with which they have invariably and skillfully executed every design transmitted from these headquarters. Brigadier-Generals Merritt and Custer, brigade commanders, have increased the confidence entertained in their ability and gallantry to lead troops on the field of battle. Colonel Devin, Sixth New York Cavalry; Colonel Gamble, Eighth Illinois; Colonel Gregg, Sixteenth Pennsylvania; Colonel Mcintosh, Third Pennsylvania; Colonel Huey, Eighth Pennsylvania Cavalry, in command of brigades, are entitled to mention for their meritorious and gallant conduct throughout the campaign."

Brig. Gen. John Buford recorded:

"July 15, the division moved to Berlin.

"July 16, moved camp to Petersville. July 17, remained at Petersville.

"July 18, crossed during the afternoon, and encamped near Purcellville.

"July 19, marched through Philomont, and encamped on Goose Creek, near Rector's Cross-Roads.

"July 20, marched to Rectortown. Detached General Merritt with his brigade to hold Manassas Gap, Gamble to hold Chester Gap, and Devin, with all the train, moved to Salem."

"... To General Merritt and Colonels Gamble and Devin, brigade commanders, I give my heartfelt thanks for their zeal and hearty support. Neither of them ever doubted the feasibility of an order, but on its reception obeyed its dictates to the letter.

"My staff—Captains [Charles E.] Norris, Keogh, [Craig W.] Wadsworth, and Bacon, and Lieutenants Mix, P. Penn Gaskill, Dean, [Albert P.] Morrow, [Malcomb H.] Wing, and [George M.] Gilchrist—were always on hand, and gave me much valuable information from where the fire was hottest, and were of immense assistance in conveying orders on the field of battle, and seeing that they were obeyed. During the campaign they were all under heavy fire on different occasions, and for coolness and gallantry cannot be excelled in this army.

"Lieutenant [Aaron B.] Jerome, signal corps, was ever on the alert, and through his intrepidity and fine glasses on more than one occasion kept me advised of the enemy's movements when no other means were available. Surgeon Hard, Eighth Illinois Cavalry, surgeon-in-chief to the division, deserve great credit for his zealous and untiring attention and labors with the sick and wounded. Through his exertions their sufferings have been greatly alleviated, their wants supplied, and many lives saved. Many wounded soldiers are indebted to him for his timely aid on the battle-field, who, but for his energy, would have shared the fate of many poor fellows who had less attentive surgeons."

Brig. Gen. George A. Custer's report detailed by each of his units:
First Michigan Cavalry
"Since the engagement at Falling Waters this regiment has been under the command of Maj. M. Brewer ..."

Fifth Michigan Cavalry
"July 17.— After sharp skirmishing with the enemy, drove them from Snicker's Gap, and occupied the same, capturing several prisoners.
"July 20.—Occupied Ashby's Gap after slight skirmishing."

Sixth Michigan Cavalry

"July 20.—The regiment participated in the capture of Ashby's Gap; also encountered the enemy strongly intrenched on the opposite side of the Shenandoah, near Berry's Ford. Loss, 3 wounded."

James Henry Avery of Custer's 5th Michigan Cavalry later wrote:

"On July 14th, we crossed the river again into Virginia, effecting the crossing just below Harper's Ferry on pontoons and took up the line of march for Snicker's Gap, where we found the rebs again and drove them out of the gap, and then moved back a short distance and went into camp. On the 19th, we were again on the road leading to Upperville, a wild mountainous route along the east side of the Blue Mountains, but, oh what nice, clear, cold springs, and what scenery; rough, but beautiful. We reached Upperville and went on picket duty for the night, forming our reserve camp, where those off duty could lie down and sleep, or tell stories." (Avery, *Under Custer's Command,* p. 45)

Brigadier General Kilpatrick, whose aggressiveness at Falling Waters resulted in heavy losses for the 6th Michigan Cavalry, impressed President Lincoln who personally ordered him to assist with the quelling of the New York City draft riots. The following is correspondence from the official records related to the New York City draft riots and the role of Brigadier General Kilpatrick during that period. (Reports of Maj. Gen. John E. Wool, U. S. Army, Commanding Department of the East, with orders, &c. JULY 13–16, 1863. Draft Riots in New York City, Troy, and Boston O.R., Series I, Vol. XXVII/2 [S# 44])

"NEW YORK CITY, *July* 17, 1863.
(Received 10.45 *a.m.)*

Major-General HALLECK,
General-in-Chief.

SIR: I think we shall put down the riot in this city in the course of this day. We had a brush with them last fight, and they were dispersed. In searching their houses, we found 70 carbines, revolvers, &c., and barrels of paving stones. The numbers of the rioters are very great, but scattered about in different parts of the city, where they plunder houses whenever the opportunity offers, in the absence of troops.

The several regiments which arrived yesterday afternoon and evening will, I trust, enable us to crush all these parties in the course of this day. The gallant and distinguished Brigadier-General Kilpatrick reported himself to me this morning for service for a few days. I have placed him in command of the few cavalry I have.

JOHN E. WOOL,
Major-General."

"New York City, July 17, 1863.

Brigadier-General CANBY,
Commanding the City:

GENERAL: I understand that you have ordered a regiment to Union Square. I think you had better send it to Madison Square. The position of Union Square is too far from the meeting. Brigadier-General Kilpatrick says that he ought to have some artillery. He will present this note to you, and will confer with you on the subject presented. I am apprehensive that we may have trouble this evening.

If proper measures are adopted and carried out, we will have no trouble to-morrow. I have great confidence in the gallant General Kilpatrick.

Very respectfully, your obedient servant,
JOHN E. WOOL,
Major-General."

In his report on the New York City riots, Major General Wool wrote: "I would also mention in terms of commendation the services of the cavalry under Colonel [Thaddeus P.] Mott, and of other cavalry of impromptu organization, and of Brigadier-General [Charles C.] Dodge, who volunteered; all of whom finally, after the dispersion of the rioters, were placed under the command of Brigadier-General [Judson] Kilpatrick, he also having volunteered. All the cavalry, however, was reserved to act under my own immediate instructions.

"On Wednesday evening, 16th instant, this cavalry was directed by me to patrol the disaffected districts, and by 9 o'clock that night they found, from the severe lessons the rioters had received at the hands of the police and troops, in killing and wounding many who were combined in arms and firing from buildings and corners upon the troops, and by the capture of many of their ringleaders, the riot had been effectually subdued.

"The last act of the tragedy was, that the cavalry, early in the morn of the 17th, found and took possession of 70 stand of revolvers and carbines, which had been secreted by the rioters in a manure heap, and several casks of paving stones, and took several prisoners.

"It will be seen that from Monday afternoon to Thursday evening the riot existed. During this period much private property was destroyed, and some public property, it is understood, was destroyed in Jamaica; also some public arms in one or two shops of individuals. The amount of private property destroyed is estimated at not less than $400,000."

Although not in the cavalry, Elisha Hunt Rhodes of Co. D, 2^d Rhode Island Volunteers, wrote about the movements of the Army of the Potomac in his diary:

"Boonsboro, Md., July 15/63—Yesterday the whole Army moved upon the Rebel's works near Hagerstown, but the enemy had fled. We followed to Williamsport, Md. where we caught about fifteen hundred prisoners who were unable to cross the river. It is said that we are to go to Berlin where we crossed last year and go into Virginia again. At last the northern soil is free from Rebels, and great must be the rejoicing at home ...

"Berlin, Md., July 17th 1863—Yesterday we again crossed the South Mountain and marching through the town of Burkittsville reached this place which is where we cross the Potomac last year. A pontoon bridge has been lain, and we shall soon cross into Virginia.

"Berlin, Md. July 19, 63—I shall regret to leave Maryland, for the country is delightful. I am almost tempted to turn farmer and move to this state. We are busy today making out our muster and pay rolls ...

"July 19th 1863—Again in Virginia. We crossed the river this afternoon and marched to this place which is called Wheatland. Here we shall camp for the night." (Rhodes, *All for the Union,* pp. 110—2)

Chapter 8

Selected Biographies

Members of the generation who led the American War for Independence from Great Britain are called the Founding Fathers. The Americans who fought in the Pacific, Europe, and served on the home front during World War II have been dubbed the Greatest Generation. The men and the women who fought and sacrificed during the bloody American Civil War for the North and the South were the members of a truly great generation also. Their beards and quaint looking uniforms often cause us to forget how very young most of them were, whether privates, generals, or, on the home front. The leaders who played a role in the Battle of Falling Waters, Maryland, were a microcosm of that great Civil War generation. Some went on to even greater success and fame after the war. Others died years later in relative obscurity with their wartime deeds their only significant impact on civilization. And still others did not outlive the war in which they served as leaders. We are left to wonder what contributions those in that last group might have made in a post-1865 United States had they survived the conflict. This question is particularly intriguing in the case of the brilliant Pettigrew who was mortally wounded during the Battle of Falling Waters on July 14, 1863.

Army of Northern Virginia

Following the Gettysburg Campaign, **Robert E. Lee** continued to lead the Army of Northern Virginia. Although his opponent was still officially George

Meade, his foe from the Gettysburg Campaign, Ulysses Grant was in overall command of the Union forces for the remaining campaigns of the war. Grant proved to be a different kind of warrior than those Lee had fought through July 1863. By 1865, Lee was General in Chief of the Armies of the Confederate States. He surrendered the Army of Northern Virginia to Grant at Appomattox, Virginia, in April 1865. Following the war, Lee served as the president of Washington College in Lexington, Virginia, which is now named Washington and Lee University. He died from a long time heart condition in Lexington, Virginia, still president of Washington College, on October 12, 1870, at age 63.

Ambrose Powell Hill remained in command of the Army of Northern Virginia's Third Corps following the Gettysburg Campaign. His subsequent battles included Bristoe Station, the Wilderness, Cold Harbor, and Petersburg. Hill was killed only days before Lee surrendered at Appomattox while leading his troops at Petersburg, Virginia, on April 2, 1865. At the time of his death, he was 39 years old.

Henry Heth remained in command of a division (Heth's Division) in Hill's Third Corps following his wounding at Gettysburg. He led his division at Bristoe Station, the Wilderness, Spotsylvania, and Petersburg. He was still serving as a division commander when Lee surrendered his army at Appomattox. Following the war Heth had an insurance business and unlike Lee, he wrote and published his memoirs. Heth died in Washington, D.C., at age 73 on September 27, 1899. History remembers Heth for having commanded the troops that fired the first shots at Gettysburg. It should be recalled his men also fired the final Confederate shots of the campaign at Falling Waters, Maryland.

James Johnson Pettigrew died from the wound he received during the battle of Falling Waters, Maryland, on July 17, 1863, in Bunker Hill, West Virginia, thirteen days after his 35th birthday. His body was transported to Raleigh, North Carolina, where it laid in state in the capitol. Following a public funeral service in Raleigh, Pettigrew's remains were transported to Bonarva, a family plantation in eastern North Carolina. Today, the land where he is buried is part of Pettigrew State Park. Pettigrew, although not well known except among the most knowledgeable Civil War historians, did gain minor acclaim again by being depicted as a bookish academic in uniform in the movie "Gettysburg." (Earl J. Hess, *Lee's Tar Heels,* p. 168)

Joseph Robert Davis, the nephew of Jefferson Davis, remained a brigadier general and continued to command a brigade for the rest of the war. After the war he worked as an attorney. Davis died at age 71 in Biloxi, Mississippi.

John Brockenbrough never again commanded a brigade following the engagement at Falling Waters. According to Bradley M. Gottfried, in his monumental work *Brigades of Gettysburg:* "Brockenbrough was relieved of his command in late July 1863, and he resumed command of the 40th Virginia. His lieutenant colonel, Henry Walker, was promoted to the rank of brigadier general, and assumed command of the consolidated brigade. Outraged, Brockenbrough resigned his commission in January 1864." (Bradley M. Gottfried, *Brigades of Gettysburg,* p. 625)

James Henry Lane continued to command the Second Brigade of Pender's Division after the Gettysburg Campaign. He was wounded at Cold Harbor. Later he commanded a brigade in Wilcox's Division at Petersburg. Lane served through the war and was at Appomattox, Virginia. Following the war he was a college professor. Lane died in Auburn, Alabama, on September 21, 1907, at age 74. Unfortunately, Lane is forgotten by history in spite of the significant role he and his men played in the Battle of Falling Waters.

Alfred Moore Scales was wounded at Gettysburg serving as a brigade commander in Pender's Division while only age 35. He went on to serve at the Wilderness and Petersburg. After the war, as a lawyer, he followed a political career and served as a U.S. congressman and as the governor of North Carolina. He died in Reidsville, North Carolina, on February 8, 1892, at age 64.

James Ewell Brown "Jeb" Stuart was mortally wounded at Yellow Tavern, Virginia, on May 12, 1864. He was only 31 years old at the time of his death. His role during the Gettysburg Campaign remains a topic of controversy and scholarly works nearly 150 years later. His dashing cavalier image remains popular in southern culture and among military history enthusiasts.

Army of the Potomac

George Gordon Meade commanded the Army of the Potomac for the rest of the conflict. In July 1863, he was promoted to the Regular Army rank of brigadier general and in 1864 he was promoted to major general in the Regular Army. He served as the commander of the Army of the Potomac for every campaign from Gettysburg through Appomattox but following the Gettysburg Campaign he served under Ulysses Grant. After the war he remained in the U. S.

Army and served as commander of the Military Division of the Atlantic and the Department of the East. Meade died in November 1872, at age 56, in his home city of Philadelphia, Pennsylvania.

The Army of the Potomac's cavalry commander, **Alfred Pleasonton,** had been promoted to major general of volunteers in June 1863, only a month prior to the Battle of Falling Waters. Following the Gettysburg Campaign he served as commander of the District of Central Missouri and the District of St. Louis. He was promoted to the rank of major general, U.S. Army, in March 1865. Pleasonton remained in the Army following the war but resigned in 1868. He died in Washington, D.C., in 1897 at age 72.

John Buford was promoted to the rank of brigadier general of volunteers in June 1863. His command of the 1st Division of the Cavalry Corps was made famous by his troopers' first contact with the Confederate forces under Henry Heth at Gettysburg. It is ironic it was also Buford's men who had the final fighting with Lee's army in the form of Heth's rear guard during the Battle of Falling Waters which concluded the Gettysburg Campaign. Disease was in fact the great killer of the Civil War. Buford died of typhoid fever in Washington, D.C., on December 16, 1863. He was only thirty-seven years old at the time of his death.

Hugh Judson "Kill Cavalry" Kilpatrick was promoted to brigadier general of volunteers in command of the 3^{d} Division of the Cavalry Corps in June 1863, similar to Buford. After the Battle of Falling Waters, he was ordered, at Lincoln's request, to report to New York City to direct military operations against the draft rioters. Later in the war, he participated in a raid on Richmond, commanded cavalry during the Atlanta Campaign, was wounded in action at Dalton, and participated in Sherman's legendary march to the sea. In June 1865, he was promoted to major general, U.S. Army. Kilpatrick served following the war as the U.S. minister to Chile. He died in Deckertown, New Jersey, in 1881 at age 45. Kilpatrick remains controversial for what is viewed as the reckless deployment and resulting slaughter of his men. This was clearly demonstrated on the battlefield at Gettysburg and later during initial charge by two companies of the 6th Michigan Cavalry at Falling Waters.

George Armstrong Custer was known at times by those familiar to him as Autie, Fanny, or Curly. He was appointed a brigadier general of volunteers in June 1863. During the Gettysburg Campaign he commanded the 2^{d} Brigade of the 3^{d} Division of the Army of the Potomac's Cavalry Corps. Following the Gettysburg Campaign, he led his horsemen in the eastern theater fighting including the Shenandoah Valley Campaign, Fisher's Hill, Five Forks, and also played a role in the final engagements leading up to Appomattox. He was promoted to major general of volunteers in October 1864, then major general, U.S. Army, in March 1865. Of all the figures who played a role at Falling Waters, none has been more celebrated in books, movies, magazines, and popular culture over the years than George Custer. Following the war he continued to serve in the U.S. Army as a lieutenant colonel in the West, fighting in the campaigns against Native Americans. He and his entire command were slaughtered at Little Big Horn, Montana, on June 25, 1876. Custer was 36 at the time of his death in battle. George Custer may have reflected on the dramatic events of July 14, 1863, at Falling Waters following the war and perhaps as he again faced overwhelming odds, this time at Little Big Horn.

All the above, except where otherwise noted, is from the Web site U.S. Civil War Generals, http://sunsite.utk.edu/civil-war/generals.html.

Although the field officers and common soldiers who fought at Falling Waters do not receive biographical treatment here, it is important to note most of the fighting and dying in all wars, including the Civil War, is done by young men (and women) whose only objective is to serve their country, remain steady under fire in front of their comrades, and return home to continue their lives. The young men in blue and gray who fought in the muddy fields and hills of western Maryland on July 14, 1863, were no different. And for this, they too deserve recognition for their courage and sacrifices. Having survived the Battle of Gettysburg, they endured the journey to western Maryland in the rain and July heat. The Battle of Falling Waters resulted in death to some of those who fought, primarily Federal cavalrymen. Others were wounded, and still others, primarily Confederates, were captured and they would endure nightmarish lives as prisoners of war in the North. Those who were not casualties went on to fight other battles, during the twenty-one months of slaughter which followed the Gettysburg Campaign. The Battle of Falling Waters, Maryland, on July 14, 1863, was a microcosm of the four year long great struggle which left blood on many farmers' fields throughout the United States of America.

Chapter 9

Post Script

(From *The Statesman-Democrat,* Martinsburg, WV, July 25, 1913)

Virginia Gets Old Banner That Was Taken By Michigan Cavalry During the War

NEW YORK, July 21 [1913]. The recent Gettysburg reunion brought out an incident which was warmly commended by the veterans of both armies, when Col. William D. Mann, of this city, returned to Governor William H. Mann, of Virginia, a flag of the Fifty-fifth Virginia Infantry.

The flag was captured by Colonel Mann's regiment, the Seventh Michigan Cavalry, from the Confederate Infantry at the battle of Falling Waters on July 14, 1863. In the engagement the flag, which bore the marks of many hard-fought battles, was gallantly defended. The Confederates were finally force to surrender, as their retreat from their position to the ford of the Potomac was cut off, and the flag fell into the hands of Colonel Mann's regiment.

Sergeant Holton took possession of the colors when the color bearer of the Fifty-fifth Virginia Infantry was struck down. He delivered the flag to Colonel Mann, who in turn delivered it to Secretary of War Stanton at the War Department in Washington. Secretary Stanton remarked that the flag had evidently been through hot fire, complimented Colonel Mann's regiment upon capturing it and then returned it to Colonel Mann with the words: "I present this to you. It will be interesting in the future of your state."

Colonel Mann carefully guarded the flag for nearly 50 years. He decided finally that he would return it to Virginia that it might be preserved among that state's trophies.

Chapter 10

Falling Waters Battlefield Today

The Antietam battlefield in Sharpsburg, Maryland, remains one of the most popular National Park Service sites among Civil War enthusiasts and historians. Unlike the more developed and commercial Gettysburg battlefield, Antietam remains to a large degree the way it was in 1862 when Lee's troops clashed with Maj. Gen. George B. McClellan's resulting in the bloodiest day in American history. The land where the July 14, 1863, Battle of Falling Waters, Maryland, was fought remains well preserved due to its rural nature, the same factor that preserved Antietam only ten miles away.

To get to the Falling Waters battlefield take exit 1 off Interstate 81, the Williamsport/Boonsboro exit, just north of the Potomac River. Once off I–81 at exit 1, follow the signs to Antietam battlefield. This will put you on Spielman Road. Off to the right as one follows Spielman Road, the old Falling Waters Road can be seen, now just an access road to a farm. It was rerouted when the interstate was built but the former narrow farm road is still clearly visible.

Driving .9 miles down Spielman Road toward Downsville (where Buford and his troopers started their day on July 14) one comes to what is now the beginning of Falling Waters Road. Take a right turn and drive down the narrow two lane farm road. One can see vast dairy farms and also many small, and in some cases ramshackle, homes on the fringe of once large farms. The hills undulate almost in a roller coaster fashion as one passes the fences, horses and cows, and "For Sale" signs.

After the turn onto Falling Waters Road, in 2.1 miles there is a church on the left and a small rise directly opposite it on the right. This is the area where Kilpatrick and his troopers formed after their mad dash from Williamsport the morning of July 14. From this point in the road, the Donnelly house is barely visible straight ahead on a rise surrounded by trees much as it was in the summer of 1863. It is from this point the two companies of Michigan cavalrymen launched their attack on Heth's position atop the ridge.

Continue on Falling Waters Road and a mixture of small homes and farmers' fields on both sides are apparent. The Daniel Donnelly house with its distinctive double chimneys is soon visible sitting atop the ridge to the right. The house and the surrounding land are private property today. No trespassing is allowed but tours of the battlefield area are offered from time-to-time. The Donnelly house property is .9 miles from the church.

From the road you can see the steep hill up which Major Weber led his two companies of Michigan horsemen to his near-certain death against Heth's rear guard. It is much steeper than imagined from descriptions and period drawings. Atop the ridge there are no remnants of the artillery lunettes which were vacant of guns on July 14. The Donnelly house, a private residence which is not open to the public, remains virtually unchanged in appearance from the time of the battle. The large German-style bank barn which stood behind and to the left of the house is long gone. Torn down following the Civil War, all that remains is the earthen ramp which now has trees growing out of the top of it. No monument stands where Pettigrew was mortally wounded but based on period accounts it is approximately halfway between the Donnelly house (which at the time of the battle had a plank fence around it) and the site of the barn. Trees and a tall hedge now cover that ground.

Across the road from the Donnelly house property are modern homes and farms. The homes sit where Brockenbrough's and Davis' men held Heth's right flank against multiple attacks, initially by Kilpatrick's and ultimately Buford's mounted troops and skirmishers on foot. It was on this ground Brockenbrough and his staff deserted their men when they withdrew to the Potomac River crossing after ordering an advance. It was on this same ground that three Virginia regimental colors were captured by the Federal horsemen.

Continue down Falling Waters Road two more miles and you will encounter the gate to the Potomac Fish and Game Club (private). The drive will give you a sense of why so many Confederates were captured between the site of the battle and the river crossing. While most modern historians refer to Heth's position as being at the bridgehead, it was in fact over two miles away at the Donnelly house and separated by hills and dense underbrush from the bridge site. It will also help you understand the painful journey that the wounded Pettigrew had to endure after being evacuated from behind the Donnelly house. At the end of Falling Waters Road is a path to the C&O Canal. At the time of this writing there is a dispute over access to the canal and the location of the Falling Waters crossing site via the path. Visitors are encouraged to contact the National Park Service for more information before attempting to access the canal site by way of this path.

Preservation efforts began when the National Park Service funded a study of the Falling Waters battlefield during the 1990s. In 2006 and 2007 the Falling Waters, Maryland, battlefield was submitted to the then Civil War Preservation Trust (CWPT), now the Civil War Trust, for most endangered status. In 2006, it was selected by the CWPT for that year's "25 Most Endangered Battlefields." While all the battlefield land currently is in private hands, work is underway with the several Civil War-focused historic land preservation organizations to protect the Falling Waters, Maryland, battlefield from further development.

Bibliography

Alexander, Gen. Edward Porter, *Military Memoirs of a Confederate*. New York: Da Capo Press, 1993.

Anders, Curt, *Henry Halleck's War, A Fresh Look at Lincoln's Controversial General-in-Chief.* Carmel, Indiana: Guild Press of Indiana, Inc., 1999.

Avery, James Henry, *Under Custer's Command,* Compiled by Karla Jean Husby, Edited by Eric J. Wittenberg. Washington, DC: Brassey's, 2000.

Blackford, Lieut. Col. W. W., C.S.A., *War Years with Jeb Stuart*. Baton Rouge: Louisiana State University Press, 1993.

Busey, John W. and David G. Marin, *Regimental Strengths and Losses at Gettysburg*. Heightstown, NJ: Longstreet House, 2005.

Carter, Lieut. Col. William R., *Sabres, Saddles and Spurs,* Edited by Col. Walbrook D. Swank. Shippensburg, PA: Burd Street Press, 1998.

Gottfried, Bradley M., *Brigades of Gettysburg.* Cambridge, MA: Da Capo Press, 2002.

Harper's Weekly, A Journal of Civilization, Vol. VII, No. 349, New York, Saturday, September 5, 1863.

Hay, John, *Inside Lincoln's White House,* Edited by Michael Burlingame and John R. Turner Ettlinger. Carbondale, IL: Southern Illinois University Press, 1977.

Hess, Earl J., *Lee's Tar Heels*. Chapel Hill, NC: The University of North Carolina Press, 2002.

Hotchkiss, Jedediah, *Make Me a Map of the Valley,* Edited by Archie P. McDonald. Dallas: Southern Methodist University Press, 1973.

Lee, Robert E., *The Wartime Papers of R. E. Lee,* Edited by Clifford Dowdey and Louis H. Manarin. New York: Bramhall House, 1961.

Miller, Francis T., editor, *The Photographic History of the Civil War,* 10 volumes, New York: Review of Reviews, 1912.

Rhodes, Elisha Hunt, *All for the Union, The Civil War Diary and Letters of Elisha Hunt Rhodes,* Edited by Robert Hunt Rhodes. New York: Vantage Books, 1985.

The Statesman-Democrat, Martinsburg, WV, July 25, 1913.

Taylor, Walter H., *General Lee, His Campaigns in Virginia, 1861–1865.* Lincoln, NE: University of Nebraska Press, 1994.

U.S. War Department, *War of the Rebellion: A Compilation of the Official Records of the Union and Confederate Armies,* 128 volumes, Washington, DC, GPO, 1880–1900.

Index

About the Author

George F. Franks, III has been passionate about the study of the American Civil War since visiting the Gettysburg battlefield with his parents in July 1963. He studied history at the U.S. Naval Academy and the University of Pittsburgh. A former telecommunications executive with extensive international experience, he is currently the president of Franks Consulting Group and the owner of CockedHats.com, a historical hat business. George is the former president of the Capitol Hill Civil War Round Table, a member of Hagerstown Civil War Round Table, Save Historic Antietam Foundation, and the Civil War Trust. He is a Governor and a former Vice President of the Company of Military Historians. George has researched the July 14, 1863 Battle of Falling Waters, Maryland, for a decade. An article he published on the battle in 2007 has grown into this book.

The Author can be reached via email at fallingwatersmd1863@gmail.com or on his Web site www.fallingwatersmd1863.com.

Made in the USA
Lexington, KY
29 January 2014